Your Career in Psychology: Psychology and the Law

TARA L. KUTHER

Western Connecticut State University

THOMSON
*
WADSWORTH

Australia • Canada • Mexico • Singapore • Spain • United Kingdom • United States

THOMSON
———★———   ™
WADSWORTH

Publisher: Vicki Knight
Acquisitions Editor: Marianne Taflinger
Editorial Assistant: Lucy Faridany
Marketing Manager: Lori Grebe
Marketing Assistant: Laurel Anderson
Print/Media Buyer: Barbara Britton

Permissions Editor: Kiely Sexton
Copy Editor: Maryann Shahidi
Cover Designer: Roger Knox
Cover Image: Christine Garrigan
Compositor: Brian May
Text and Cover Printer: Webcom

Printed in Canada
1 2 3 4 5 6 7 07 06 05 04 03

For more information about our products, contact us at:
Thomson Learning Academic Resource Center
1-800-423-0563
For permission to use material from this text, contact us by:
Phone: 1-800-730-2214
Fax: 1-800-730-2215

Web: http://www.thomsonrights.com

Library of Congress Control Number: 2003112636

ISBN 0-534-61779-4

Wadsworth/Thomson Learning
10 Davis Drive
Belmont, CA 94002-3098
USA

Asia
Thomson Learning
5 Shenton Way #01-01
UIC Building
Singapore 068808

Australia/New Zealand
Thomson Learning
102 Dodds Street
Southbank, Victoria 3006
Australia

Canada
Nelson
1120 Birchmount Road
Toronto, Ontario M1K 5G4
Canada

Europe/Middle East/Africa
Thomson Learning
High Holborn House
50/51 Bedford Row
London WC1R 4LR
United Kingdom

Latin America
Thomson Learning
Seneca, 53
Colonia Polanco
11560 Mexico D.F.
Mexico

Spain/Portugal
Paraninfo
Calle/Magallanes, 25
28015 Madrid, Spain

Tara L. Kuther, Ph.D. is Associate Professor of psychology at Western Connecticut State University, where she teaches courses in child, adolescent, and adult development. She values opportunities to conduct collaborative research with students and is active in the Council for Undergraduate Research as Psychology Councilor. Dr. Kuther is Chair of the Instructional Resource Award Task Force of the Office of Teaching Resources in Psychology (OTRP) of the Society for Teaching of Psychology, Division 2 of the American Psychological Association. She has taught both undergraduate and graduate courses at a wide range of institutions, including Lehman College (CUNY), Fordham University, and Teachers College, Columbia University. Her research examines risky behavior during adolescence and young adulthood, moral development, and ethics in research and teaching. She is the author of *The Psychology Major's Handbook,* and coauthor of *Careers in Psychology: Opportunities in a Changing World*. To learn more about Dr. Kuther's research, visit her website at *http://tarakuther.com*

Brief Contents

Contents

Chapter 3

Correctional and Police Psychology   29

Chapter 4

Consulting   41

Preface

Many psychology students are fascinated by the interplay between psychology and law--so much so that courses in legal and forensic psychology are popular among students in nearly every psychology department. Despite the popularity of legal and forensic psychology, many misconceptions persist about careers in psychology and law.

My goal in writing this book is to introduce students to the variety of forms that legal and forensic psychology careers may take and to dispel pervasive myths. Each chapter presents a career path, including an overview, advantages and disadvantages, and a profile of a psychologist who has chosen that path. Consider this book a starting point for exploring legal and forensic careers in psychology. Discuss the career opportunities presented within these pages with your advisor and psychology professors.

Your Career in Psychology: Psychology and Law begins by discussing the nature of legal and forensic psychology and the diverse career paths available in this field. Chapter 2 explores the role of psychologists in conducting forensic evaluations for the court. Careers in correctional and police psychology are presented in Chapter 3. Psychologists' consulting roles as trial consultants, mediators, and expert witnesses are discussed in Chapter 4. Psychologists often conduct social policy-related research and serve as congressional fellows and staff members, as presented in Chapter 5. The final chapter of this book explores graduate training in psychology and law and discusses what you can do now, as an undergraduate to prepare and advance your career.

ACKNOWLEDGMENTS

This book was not a solitary endeavor, but benefited from the assistance, feedback, and support from of many. I am most appreciative of the constructive comments and helpful suggestions that I received from reviewers: Lawrence Wrightsman, University of Kansas, Edie Greene, University of Colorado-Colorado Springs, Michael Nietzel, Dean at the University of Kentucky, and Mark Costanzo of Claremont Graduate School.

I thank Marianne Taflinger for taking this project under her wing, guiding it through the review and revision process, and sharing her expertise. Thanks for to Vicki Knight for identifying the promise of this project and directing it to the appropriate channels to make it happen. Robert Morgan encouraged me to take on this project and was always there to hear ideas and answer questions--thanks. Several professionals took time from their busy schedules to be profiled for this book: Karen Franklin, Eric Mart, Robert Morgan, Evan Nelson, and Scyatta Wallace. Thank you for contributing your time, advice, and insight. Thanks to Terrence DeMay and Lawrence Wrightsman for granting permission to reprint their profiles. Finally, I thank my family:–my parents, Philip and Irene Kuther, and my husband, Larry DeCarlo–for their unwavering support through the years.

Tara L. Kuther

INTRODUCTION TO PSYCHOLOGY AND LAW

CHAPTER GUIDE

The psychologist arrives at the crime scene and examines the clues to learn about and identify with the individual who committed the horrendous act. Conducting interviews to understand the offender's life and ultimately assist in his or her pursuit and capture— certainly this scenario represents the interface of psychology and law, right? Popular films and television shows like *Silence of the Lambs*, *CSI*, and *Profiler* depict forensic psychology as an action-packed career of profiling dangerous criminals. Though the popular press and media portrayals lead many students to believe that forensic psychology and careers in psychology and law make for exciting adventures, similar to those on television and in the movies, this is rarely the case (Kuther & Morgan, 2004). So then, what is psychology and law? Let's take a look at some of the ways in which these two fields intersect, as illustrated by the many roles of psychologists with interests in the law:

- Assessing juror competence
- Using psychological techniques to determine which jurors might act favorably towards a defendant
- Analyzing the reliability of eyewitness testimony
- Assessing the capacity of a defendant to stand trial
- Determining appropriate interventions and treatments for criminal offenders
- Conducting a risk assessment to determine whether an individual poses a risk to society
- Designing social support and other programs to assist law enforcement officers with stress management, coping skills, and crisis management
- Conducting a survey to determine the public's general knowledge about a particular case to support a change-of-venue request
- Assisting legislators in understanding psychological phenomena that pertain to legal issues

Large numbers of students express interest in pursuing careers in psychology and law (Kuther & Morgan, 2004). But there's a great deal of misinformation about what such careers entail. This book will explore the full range of careers in psychology and law.

AN OVERVIEW OF PSYCHOLOGY AND LAW

Although they are distinct fields, both psychology and law seek to improve the quality of human life. Psychology improves our quality of life by increasing our understanding of people and promoting optimal human development and function. The law delineates a governing body and set of rules to live by so that we may all coexist harmoniously and equally. Psychology's role in the legal system is to "ensure that laws reflect basic human values" and to assess the validity of the assumptions about human nature and behavior that are inherent in laws (Ogloff, Beavers, & DeLeon, 1999, p. 331).

As Ogloff (1999) explains, because "every law has as its purpose the control or regulation of human behavior, every law is ripe for psychological study"(Ogloff, 1999, pp. 2–3). The legal system provides psychologists with many opportunities for research and practice.

Forensic Evaluation

Some psychologists conduct forensic evaluations for use within civil or criminal court cases. In civil court cases, individuals bring forth a suit to resolve a dispute between two parties or because they believe that someone has physically or emotionally injured them (Huss, 2001). A worker's compensation case or personal injury suit might require a psychologist to determine the extent of emotional harm suffered by the plaintiff. Psychologists assess the emotional impact of traumatic injury, including post-traumatic stress, depression, chronic pain, or anxiety. If a head injury is present, psychologists may conduct a neuropsychological assessment to evaluate memory dysfunction and cognitive impairments that coincide with the injuries. Psychologists may also be asked to evaluate the long-term emotional impact of traumatic events, such as the effect of a child of losing his/her mother, or the effects of criminal victimization. Within the context of a life insurance claim case, a psychologist might provide expert analysis of whether an accidental death was a disguised suicide. Psychologists advise child custody cases by evaluating parental competence and emotional stability, and determining what custody arrangement is best for the children.

Criminal court cases are those in which an individual has committed a crime against society (Huss, 2001). Psychologists might be called on in criminal cases to provide testimony on whether an individual is competent to stand trial, to discuss the defendant's psychological state at the time the crime occurred, or assess the potential for future violence during a sentencing hearing. Forensic evaluations may be conducted to determine the presence of psychological problems that may have influenced the crime; sentencing and probation decisions often are informed by forensic evaluations.

Research

Many psychologists conduct research that holds implications for the law. Some study the validity and limits of eyewitness testimony. Others examine factors that influence the credibility of testimony and how to appropriately interview witnesses (i.e., without coercing or contaminating their testimony). Prominent research areas within the field of psychology and law include: juror selection, eyewitness testimony, the relation of mental illness and violence, forensic assessment and treatment issues, the effectiveness of trial consultants and their influence on juries, and evaluations of the impact of laws on behavior (e.g., whether changes in the legal drinking age influence rates of alcohol consumption by young people).

Treatment

Psychologists provide counseling and psychotherapy, and assist in program development and evaluation within the criminal justice system, including correctional and police settings. Psychologists who work in correctional settings engage in direct service delivery by conducting psychological assessments as inmates enter the prison system, preventing, diagnosing, and treating mental disorders, providing basic mental health services to inmates, and engaging in crisis management (Boothby & Clements, 2000; Milan, Chin, & Nguyen, 1999).

Police psychologists provide a variety of evaluative, counseling, training, and support services to police agencies. They select and train police officers, conduct fitness for duty and special unit evaluations, engage in field consultations (e.g., assisting in the apprehension or security of a mentally ill person), provide organizational development and support, and counsel officers and their families to help them cope with the stressful lifestyle a career in law enforcement entails   (Bartol, 1996; Bergen, Aceto, & Chadziewicz, 1992; Scrivner & Kurke, 1995; Super, 1999). Both police and correctional psychologists develop and evaluate programs to address the wide variety of client and organizational needs.

Consulting

Some psychologists with legal and forensic interests develop careers in consulting, specifically trial consulting, mediation, or expert witnessing. Trial consultants assist attorneys in preparing for, and carrying out, trials. They assess the general public's perceptions, knowledge, and biases about a given case, provide advice about jury selection, trial strategy, and presentation, and assist lawyers in preparing witnesses for examination during the trial. Other psychologists act as mediators, or third parties who assist disputants in reconciling their civil court cases in order to avoid trial (Wrightsman, 2001). Finally, psychologists may serve as expert witnesses as part of an attorney's presentation of the evidence during a trial. Psychologists might testify about their forensic evaluation, or their applied research that pertains to the court case. Here, the expert witness provides testimony that explains complicated psychological issues to help the jurors to understand the issues and uncover the truth.

Public Policy and Social Advocacy

Many psychologists conduct policy-related research, or research that sheds light on important social problems (e.g., the impact of welfare reform on low-income families). Policy-minded psychologists lobby and inform legislators about their research findings as well as other relevant findings. Psychologists can become involved in politics by working with members of Congress as Congressional Fellows (a specialized fellowship to introduce psychologists to politics and political life, discussed in Chapter 5) or as staff members. These psychologists develop briefs, conduct psycholegal research, and become involved in planning and drafting laws (American Psychological Association, 2002).

Political consultants conduct surveys to gather information about public opinions, provide advice about how to address volatile issues that affect voters, and guide political campaigns. Finally, psychologists have run for office and become politicians in state legislatures and even the U.S. Congress (Sullivan, 2001).

CURRENT ISSUES IN PSYCHOLOGY AND LAW

Psychology and law is a growth field. Over the past three decades, many psychology and law journals have begun publication, including *Law and Human Behavior, Behavioral Sciences and the Law, Criminal Justice and Behavior, Journal of Forensic Psychology Practice,* and *Psychology, Public Policy, and the Law,* which is both a psychology and a legal journal. Psychology and law has its own professional organizations (American Academy of Forensic Psychology, American Association of Correctional Psychologists, and American College of Forensic Psychology), and approximately 3,000 psychologists are members of the American Psychology-Law Society (APLS; Division 41 of the American Psychological Association) (Otto & Heilbrun, 2002). Psychology and law has emerged as a field of study within clinical and counseling psychology programs, as a stand-alone program, as well as joint-degree programs offering degrees in law and doctorates in psychology (for more information about graduate study in psychology and law, see Chapter 6).

Although it is a distinct field of study, there is controversy as to how to define the scope of psychology and law, and more specifically, forensic psychology (Brigham, 1999). As we've seen, psychologists serve a variety of functions within the legal system. Some theorists argue that the entire field of psychology and law can be referred to as forensic psychology (Bartol & Bartol, 1999; Hess, 1999; Wrightsman, 2001). For example, Wrightsman (2001) offers a broad definition: "Forensic psychology is reflected by any application of psychological knowledge or methods to a task faced by the legal system" (p. 2). Hess (1999) adds, "Psychology in the law, psychology by the law, and psychology of the law comprise forensic psychology" (p. 5).

Other professionals define forensic psychology more narrowly to specifically describe the clinical practice of psychology within legal contexts. For example, the American Board of Forensic Psychology and the American Psychology-Law Society (1995) define forensic psychology as:

> the professional practice by psychologists within the areas of clinical psychology, counseling psychology, neuropsychology, and school psychology, when they are engaged regularly as experts and represent themselves as such, in an activity primarily intended to provide professional psychological expertise to the judicial system. (p. 6)

Narrow definitions limit the scope of forensic psychology to clinical and professional practice issues including assessing cognitive competence, determining a defendant's mental state at the time of the crime, and other activities that require training in clinical and counseling areas of psychology. Critics argue that narrow definitions of forensic psychology exclude many functions that psychologists serve in the legal system, including evaluation-research, trial consulting and expert testimony (Wrightsman, 2001). Nevertheless, this narrow practice-related definition of forensic psychology has been accepted and conferred specialty status by the American Psychological Association (APA), meaning that graduate training programs can now seek specialty designations as forensic psychology programs (American Psychological Association, 2001).

Given the APA's designation of forensic psychology as a clinical practice specialty, we will define forensic psychology narrowly in this book to refer to the clinical practice of psychology within legal settings (e.g., forensic evaluation and treatment). The evaluation-research, trial consultant, and expert testimony activities of psychologists will be referred to as legal psychology. Therefore, the field of psychology and the law entails two broad divisions (Brigham, 1999): forensic psychology (the practice of assessment and treatment activities within a legal setting) and legal psychology (the intersection of psychological research and the legal system, including trial consultation and expert testimony).

Throughout this book we will explore the applied activities of forensic and legal psychologists. However, most psychologists, regardless of specialty, engage in multiple roles. In other words a forensic psychologist might engage in forensic evaluations (see Chapter 2), provide expert testimony (see Chapter 4), conduct research on legal issues, and teach courses in forensic psychology. Before we discuss the varied applied activities of forensic and legal psychologists, let's examine their roles in academia.

FORENSIC AND LEGAL PSYCHOLOGISTS IN ACADEMIA

Academic careers for legal and forensic psychologists are not limited to departments of psychology. These specialists work as professors in departments of criminal justice and social science, as well as in law schools. As another example, a psychologist who specializes in legal issues that arise in industrial/organizational psychology (e.g., sexual harassment or white-collar crime) may work in a school of business.

Scope of the Professorial Career

Despite the different types of academic institutions (community colleges, 4-year colleges and universities, and research-oriented universities), all academic careers share certain features. As you consider a career as a professor, recognize that there is more to the professorate than lecturing in front of a class (Kuther & Morgan, 2004). Before a professor steps into the classroom, a great deal of time and effort has gone into preparation. Each lecture requires background reading of chapters and journal articles in addition to the text, note taking, and preparation of overheads, activities, and discussion questions. This work is never finished because even experienced professors must update their notes to remain current with the ever-changing field (Roediger, 1997). A professor's teaching activities extend beyond the classroom to include grading, meeting with students to answer questions and discuss course content and professional issues, advising students on career choices, and writing student recommendation letters.

In addition to teaching, professorial careers entail many roles, usually including conducting research and providing service to the campus and community. During a typical week, professors often divide their time among multiple research tasks including working on an article or book, conducting statistical analyses, planning research, writing grant proposals, searching the literature, reading research articles, meeting with student research assistants, advising students on their research, and preparing or giving talks at professional meetings. Professors also participate in faculty meetings as well as the many committees that administrate and run the university. Many forensic and legal psychology faculty also engage in applied activities, such as consulting work (e.g., conducting forensic evaluations or providing expert testimony).

Advantages and Disadvantages of a Career as a Professor

Some of the greatest advantages that college professors enjoy are academic freedom, and the autonomy and flexibility of academic life; they may "teach the truth as they see it" (Vesilind, 2000, p. 10). In other words, professors decide on the best methods to teach their courses. Texts, reading assignments, grading, and evaluation procedures often are up to the professor. Professors also are autonomous in conducting their research. By writing and winning research grants, professors obtain funding to study problems of their choosing. Through research, and scholarly publication professors gain opportunities for travel and contact with the public through speaking at conferences and writing for the popular press. Flexibility is an important benefit of a career as a professor. Outside of class, professors' schedules tend to be flexible. Most professors develop work habits that fit their lives; allowing time to pick up children from school, spend time with their families, and complete preparation and writing activities at other times of the day, such as the late evenings or early mornings.

Another advantage is tenure. Tenure is a permanent job contract, gained after a probationary period of six or seven years. Professors with documented teaching histories, excellent student evaluations, publications, campus committee work, and outreach to the community cab earn tenure and, therefore, job security. Tenure guarantees that faculty who have demonstrated their effectiveness as teachers and scholars cannot be dismissed for political reasons like holding and teaching unpopular views, being critical of the college's administration, or pursuing controversial research. Tenure ensures that universities remain safe havens for intellectual pursuit and the development of new ideas, which brings us to the other benefits of the professorate: the excitement of discovery and innovation, as well as rewards of imparting knowledge and introducing students to a life of the mind (Roediger, 1997; Vesilind, 2000). Professors have the opportunity to work with information that they love and share it with students. That is perhaps the best benefit of all.

Like all careers, the professorate also entails disadvantages, the primary one being the scarcity of positions. The academic job market is very competitive. Some applicants spend several years working as postdoctoral researchers, in one-year instructor appointments, or in adjunct positions (teaching part-time, often at several colleges at once). Applicants must also be prepared to seek faculty positions in a variety of geographic locations, not just only one place.

Once a position is obtained, new professors juggle many demands. In addition to teaching loads and service responsibilities, new faculty members are expected to begin a research program because in recent years research has increased in importance— even for those in primarily undergraduate teaching-oriented colleges (Salzinger, 1995). Professorial careers entail long hours because faculty are expected to do it all: teach well, publish in the best journals, bring in grant monies to fund research and graduate students, and serve the university and community. These multiple pressures can be very stressful for new faculty who are just learning the full capacity of their professor role and acclimating themselves to university life.

Finally, professors' salaries allow for a comfortable life, but certainly not a rich one. A beginning professor, called an assistant professor, earns on average between $42,000 and $53,000 annually, varying by institution, whereas a full professor (a senior-level position) earns on average between $64,000 and $90,000 (Chronicle of Higher Education, 2001).

OVERVIEW OF THIS BOOK

Each chapter in this book discusses a different career path within legal and forensic psychology. Chapter 2 discusses the field of forensic evaluation and the consultant activities of forensic psychologists. In Chapter 3, you'll learn about careers in correctional and forensic psychology. Many psychologists act as consultants; Chapter 4 discusses trial consultants, and psychologists as mediators and expert witnesses. Social activism often is associated with psychology. Chapter 5 explores policy-related activities of psychologists in academia, government, and nonprofit agencies, as well as psychologists who have embarked on careers as political consultants. Finally, Chapter 6 provides guidance on training for a career in legal or forensic psychology. You'll learn about the various training paths and what you can do now to prepare for a career in psychology and law.

SUGGESTED READINGS

Arrigo, B. A. (2000). *Introduction to forensic psychology: Issues and controversies in crime and justice.* San Diego, CA: Academic Press.

Huss, M. T. (2001). Psychology and law, now and in the next century: The promise of an emerging area of psychology. In J. S. Halonen & S. F. Davis (Eds.), *The many faces of psychological research in the 21st Century.* Society for the Teaching of Psychology. Retrieved from http://teachpsych.lemoyne.edu/teachpsych/faces/text/Ch11.htm

Huss, M. T. (2001). What is forensic psychology? *It's not Silence of the Lambs! Eye on Psi Chi, 5*(3), 25-27. Retrieved on June 18, 2003, at http://www.psichi.org/content/publications/eye/volume/vol_5/5_3/huss.asp

Kuther, T. L. (2003). *The psychology major's handbook.* Pacific Grove, CA: Wadsworth.

Kuther, T. L., & Morgan, R. (2004). *Extending the boundaries of psychology: Career opportunities in a changing world.* Pacific Grove, CA: Wadsworth.

Vesilind, P. A. (2000). *So you want to be a professor? A handbook for graduate students.* Thousand Oaks, CA: Sage.

Wrightsman, L. S. (2001). *Forensic psychology.* Belmont, CA: Wadsworth.

WEB RESOURCES

American Psychology-Law Society
http://www.unl.edu/ap-ls/

Careers in Psychology and Law
http://www.unl.edu/ap-ls/careers.htm

PsychLaw.org
http://www.psyclaw.org/

Forensic Psychology
    http://faculty.ncwc.edu/toconnor/425/425lect18.htm
Forensic Psychology Careers and Training
    http://psychology.about.com/cs/lawcareer/index.htm
Careers in Forensic Psychology
    http://www.wcupa.edu/_ACADEMICS/sch_cas.psy/Career_Paths/Forensic/
    Career08.htm

PROFILE 1.1 : LAWRENCE WRIGHTSMAN, JR., PH.D.

Dr. Lawrence Wrightsman is a Professor of Social Psychology at the University of Kansas who specializes in forensic psychology. He is the author or coauthor of 40 books and more than 70 articles and book chapters. In addition to authoring one of the leading forensic psychology textbooks, Dr. Wrightsman maintains an active research program that focuses on judicial decision making, the comparison of judge and jury verdicts, and police interrogations and jurors' reactions to confessions. Dr. Wrightsman has received many awards and honors, including a 1998 Distinguished Career Award from the American Psychology-Law Society (American Psychological Association Division 41).

Dr. Wrightsman provided responses to several questions we posed concerning his background and assessment of the field of forensic psychology.

What originally got you interested in the field of forensic psychology?

I was trained as a social psychologist and around the mid-1970s began doing research on psychology-and-law topics (as a number of social psychologists did at that time). I have always been intrigued with the courtroom and the jury trial—two versions of the truth always zealously and usually sincerely portrayed, but only one can be true.

From the early 1980s to the present, I have taught courses on psychology and the law, jury behavior, judicial decision making, and similar topics. About five years ago, I noticed undergraduate students were increasingly coming to my office, wanting to become "forensic psychologists." This term was just beginning to surface to in the public's consciousness, mainly as a result of the movie *Silence of the Lambs*. Suddenly, young people wanted to be criminal profilers like Jodie Foster was in the movie.

So, I began to explore just what was "forensic psychology." I began to teach a graduate-level course on the topic (which draws 40–50 students every time it is offered). The term remains vague and controversial; I prefer to think of it as any application of psychological concepts or findings to the legal system, but others want to restrict it to the clinical/practitioner activities. I am currently completing a forensic psychology textbook (for Brooks/Cole-Wadsworth), which will be the first of its kind. So I suppose I am a "forensic psychologist," although I am not a clinical psychologist and hence am not eligible for ABEPP or similar fellow status.

Describe what activities you are involved in as a forensic psychologist.

In addition to teaching, I am occasionally involved in trial consultation. For example, I carry out change-of-venue surveys when a criminal defendant claims that pretrial publicity in the local area means that he/she cannot get a fair trial there. I also serve as an expert witness, especially on the accuracy of eyewitness identification or the validity of confessions. (These are topics that I believe reflect "forensic psychology," although the basis for the testimony comes from experimental, not clinical, psychology).

What are your particular areas of expertise or interest?

As I indicated, any topic dealing with an application of psychology to the courtroom. Recently, I analyzed a number of the amicus briefs submitted by the American Psychological Association to the Supreme Court.

What are some future trends you see in forensic psychology?

Currently, there is more demand from students than there are programs. Fewer than ten schools offer a program clearly labeled as Forensic Psychology, and some of these are too new to be accredited by APA. One freestanding professional school now offers such a program, and I expect others to follow.

The issue remains, should forensic psychology seek specialty status by APA, as clinical, school, and counseling psychology have done? And if it does, should it be only clinical-practitioner based, or is there room for the experimental psychologist who serves as an expert witness or survey consultant? The field is struggling over this issue right now.

(from Trull & Phares, 2001)

PROFILE 1.2 : ROBERT D. MORGAN, PH.D.

Dr. Robert D. Morgan is an assistant professor at Texas Tech University who specializes in forensic psychology. He received his B.S. in Psychology from University of Nebraska–Kearney, M.S. in Clinical Psychology from Fort Hays State University, and Ph.D. in Counseling Psychology from Oklahoma State University. His first experiences with forensic psychology were early in his career. Before earning his Ph.D., he worked for two years as a mental health professional in correctional facilities in Kansas. Dr. Morgan completed a predoctoral internship at the Federal Correctional Institution in Petersburg, Virginia, and a postdoctoral fellowship in forensic psychology at the Department of Psychiatry, University of Missouri–Kansas City Medical School, in conjunction with the Missouri Department of Mental Health.

Dr. Morgan provided responses to several questions I posed concerning his background and assessment of the field of forensic psychology.

How did you become interested in forensic psychology?

My interest in forensic psychology began with a master's level internship during my training at Fort Hays State University. We had to complete a 3-month internship and I realized that I needed experience with diverse populations. Growing up in Nebraska in a white, middle-class family resulted in a somewhat sheltered life, and I thought I needed more experience with diverse groups to broaden my horizons and become a better therapist. I couldn't afford to move, so I thought that a prison setting would offer experiences that would broaden my horizons. I contacted the Chief Psychologist (Donald Denney, Ph.D.) at the U.S. Federal Penitentiary at Leavenworth, Kansas, and asked him if I could work there for a summer. After convincing him that he wouldn't have to pay me, he agreed and I worked there for 10 weeks providing psychological services. I loved the work, which led me to accept a master's-level position in the Kansas Department of Corrections after I graduated from Fort Hays State. My interests broadened from strictly correctional psychology to forensic psychology during my graduate work at OSU and even more so during my predoctoral internship.

Describe what forensic activities you are involved in as a forensic psychologist.

My current forensic activities are limited to criminal forensic work (I don't do child custody cases, personal injury litigation, etc.). In other words, I conduct court ordered evaluations on persons charged with a crime (i.e., defendants) and the evaluation questions are typically regarding competency to stand trial and/or criminal responsibility. My full-time job is in academia where I do offender-based research (e.g., treatment efficacy, effects of imprisonment on offenders), so my private practice is part time.

When doing an evaluation I spend anywhere from 2-10 hours with a defendant whereby I'll do a clinical interview, mental status examination, and psychological testing (if warranted). Then I'll spend an hour or two analyzing data, scoring test data, and so on, and then 2–3 hours writing a report that gets sent to the court. As Texas is a large state, it is common for me to travel to other towns/counties to do an evaluation. Also, I occasionally testify about the results of my examinations or about the opinions I have provided the court in my report.

What are your specialties and areas of expertise?

My areas of expertise are primarily in criminal forensic work with particular interest in competency issues, criminal responsibility, and risk assessment/dangerousness.

Describe advantages and disadvantages to a career in forensic psychology.

I have heard forensic psychology described as a "sexy" profession and this is true as there is potential to earn a large income, as well the professional recognition that comes with forensic work in high-profile cases. How often do psychologists normally get to see their name in the paper? However, more importantly for most professionals is the opportunity and professional satisfaction of assisting the court and helping in the determination of the type of services one receives.

Disadvantages include the stress of cross-examination and going to court in general. One recent trial I was involved in required that I drive two hours to get there. It was a very high profile case and I was so nervous I thought I might be sick along the way. Envision a psychologist pulling over and being sick on the side of the road—in a new suit! That's the stress of court testimony for neophytes such as myself. In addition, we are often involved in cases that significantly impact people's life, some that include decisions of life and death. I felt uneasy when the case I was recently involved in resulted in a verdict for the death penalty. Although I didn't make that decision, I certainly played a role in the process. A final disadvantage is the need to avoid the temptation to offer opinions based on what attorneys want. This is a business and it's tempting to want to give the consumer (i.e., attorney) what he or she wants, but objectivity is the key to the profession, thus you must consciously avoid the desire to be helpful and remain true to the data (i.e., nobody wants to be a psychological whore).

What advice would you give to a student considering a career in forensic psychology?

Pursue training in a generalist program (i.e., clinical or counseling psychology) with particular interest in programs that have faculty conducting research or working in correctional/forensic psychology. Then pursue specialty training during graduate school or internship/postdoc. Get involved in research that works with issues that are related to forensic work such as violence/aggression, domestic abuse, offender/inmate research, and so on. Seek to increase your knowledge of the issues that are central to offenders' lives. In addition, students should seek alternative learning experiences. For example, go to court and observe the court process, expert witnesses, and so on.

FORENSIC EVALUATION AND THE COURT

CHAPTER GUIDE

Psychological and mental health issues frequently emerge within legal contexts. It is estimated that mental-health professionals participate as experts in about one-million court cases per year (O'Connor, Sales & Schulman, 1996). Forensic psychologists may work as consulting experts in court cases, conducting assessments and working behind the scenes to gather data to support a case, or they may provide testimony as expert witnesses (Ogloff & Cronshaw, 2001). This chapter explores the consultative emphasis of forensic psychologists as forensic evaluators (see Chapter 4 for a discussion of the forensic psychologist as expert witness).

FORENSIC EVALUATION

Forensic psychologists often are called on to conduct psychological evaluations of individuals in preparation for both criminal and civil court cases. After conducting evaluations, forensic psychologists write comprehensive reports documenting their findings. The reports inform the court about important psychological issues, such as a defendant's mental state at the time of the crime, whether a defendant is competent for trial, or whether a plaintiff's injuries suggest malingering (falsification). Reports may be delivered to the court, to the client directly, or to the attorney. In some jurisdictions, the psychologist must be present in court to answer questions about the report in order for it to be considered evidence (Walker, 1990). The following sections consider the range of assessment activities in which forensic psychologists engage.

Criminal Cases

Psychological evaluations offer critical information within criminal court cases. For example, consider a criminal case in which an adolescent defendant with a history of physical abuse is accused of murder. A forensic psychologist might be called upon to determine whether neurological damage extending from the physical abuse may have impaired the adolescent's judgment and impulse control. In this case, a forensic neuropsychologist may conduct a comprehensive evaluation of brain functioning to measure deficits that may influence psychological functioning and behavior. Some of the psychological issues that forensic psychologists evaluate include criminal responsibility; adjudicative competence; victim trauma and injury; and veracity of child abuse allegations.

Criminal responsibility. At the time of the offense, was the defendant aware of the implications of his or her actions? Frequently forensic psychologists are called on to evaluate whether a defendant was insane at the time of the crime. Determining insanity is extraordinarily difficult because it entails making a retrospective statement of the person's mental state at the time of the crime, often committed months or years before the forensic evaluation (Wrightsman, 2001).

Typically, interview-based instruments are used in the forensic evaluation. For example, the Rogers Criminal Responsibility Assessment Scales (Rogers, 1984) are designed to quantify the legal definition of insanity into a series of items that assist in determining whether the individual was incompetent at the time of the offense. In his or her report, the forensic psychologist explains how psychopathological processes experienced at the time of the crime may have influenced the defendant's perceptions, cognitions, objectives, impulse control, and ultimate actions (Ogloff, Roberts, & Roesch, 1993). The forensic psychologist must also indicate the limits to his or her conclusions as well sources of error, such as examiner bias or possible malingering on the part of the defendant (Wrightsman, 2001).

Adjudicative competence. Perhaps the most common activity of forensic psychologists within criminal court cases is determining adjudicative competence, or a defendant's capacity to understand the legal proceedings and function meaningfully within the court setting (Wrightsman, Greene, Neitzel, & Fortune, 2002). Is the defendant competent to stand trial? Is the defendant competent to plead guilty and waive his or her constitutional rights including the right to a jury trial and to confront his accusers? Does the defendant have the adjudicative capacity to waive his or her right to an attorney and instead represent him or herself at trial? If the defendant is a minor, does he or she have the cognitive capacity to meaningfully participate in the legal proceedings?

An evaluation of competence entails assessing foundational and decisional competence (Wrightsman et al., 2002). Foundational competence refers to the ability to: understand the legal system and process, including the adversarial nature of the legal process; communicate meaningfully with his or her attorney; and understand the situation at hand. Decisional competence refers to an individual's capacity to understand the information presented and make rational choices regarding the various legal alternatives that are in his or her best interests.

To evaluate competence, the forensic psychologist conducts interviews with the defendant and administers psychological tests that are designed to assess competency, such as the Competency Screening Test (Lipsitt, Lelos, & McGarry, 1971), Competency Assessment Instrument (Laboratory for Community Psychiatry, 1974), and MacArthur Measures of Competence (Hoge et al., 1997). The forensic psychologist then writes a report communicating the methods used and conclusions drawn regarding the defendant's adjudicative competence, as well as the limitations of the methods and potential sources of error, such as malingering or instrumentation issues.

Victim trauma and injury. Forensic psychologists frequently play a role in evaluating the effects of trauma and/or injuries on victims. For example, a forensic psychologist may evaluate a rape victim to (1) document symptoms of rape trauma syndrome; (2) document psychological functioning before and after the assault; and (3) determine social adjustment and coping after the assault (Wrightsman, 2001). Several instruments may be used in assessing rape victims, such as the Sexual Assault Symptoms Scale (Ruch, Gartrell, Amedeo, & Coyne, 1991), Rape Trauma Symptom Rating Scale (DiVasto, 1985), and Clinical Trauma Assessment (Ruch, Gartrell, Ramelli, & Coyne, 1991). Similar assessments may occur in cases of child abuse: to determine the extent of the psychological and developmental trauma to the child. After the trauma assessment, the forensic psychologist explains the evaluation methods, findings, conclusions, and limitations in a written report.

Veracity of child abuse allegations. In cases of alleged child abuse, forensic psychologists evaluate the victim and assess his or her competence to testify. This entails determining whether the child understands the difference between truth and falsehood, has the ability to remember and describe the event in question, and has the social skills to testify in court. Forensic psychologists interview children who allege physical or sexual abuse. The content of children's reports are analyzed by applying a variety of criteria to distinguish truthful allegations from fantasy (e.g., Marxsen, Yuille, & Nisbet, 1995) and the results are reported to the court. As in other types of forensic evaluations, the methods, results, conclusions, and limitations of the assessment are communicated in reports written by the forensic psychologist.

Civil Cases

Civil court cases also rely on evaluations conducted by forensic psychologists. These evaluations can include issues of child custody, competency, civil commitment, psychological damages, and physical autopsy.

Child custody evaluations. Child custody cases are among the fastest growing areas of forensic psychological assessment. In these cases, forensic psychologists must evaluate families and recommend the custodial arrangement that is in the best interests of the child. The forensic psychologist evaluates the child's wishes, parents' wishes, relationships among the family members, mental health and parenting competence of the adults, and the child's adjustment and developmental needs (American Psychological Association, 1994). After interviewing, testing, and observing the family members in interactions, as well as interviewing persons close to the family and examining relevant records of family members (e.g., school records, medical records, arrest records), the forensic psychologist writes a report communicating the evaluation methods, findings, conclusions, limitations, and recommendations on the custody arrangement that will best promote the child's welfare (Bow & Quinnell, 2001).

Competency evaluations. Is this older adult competent to prepare a will or to manage his or her financial affairs? Can this adolescent make competent decisions regarding medical or psychiatric treatment? Is the individual competent to draw up a living will? Forensic psychologists assess the decisional competence of individuals. The assessment entails determining whether the individual is capable of understanding information relevant to the decision, anticipating potential consequences of each alternative, rationally weighing the costs and benefits of each alternative to arrive at a decision, and communicating that decision to relevant persons (e.g., physician, attorney) (Appelbaum & Grisso, 1995). Varying techniques are used to assess competency; however, there is no standard assessment instrument to determine competency (Kuther, 1999), making such assessments quite difficult.

Civil commitment. Is the individual a danger to him or herself? Does he or she require hospitalization for mental health treatment? Is the individual dangerous to others? Must this person receive mandatory mental health treatment within an outpatient setting? Answering each of these questions requires a forensic evaluation. Forensic psychologists interview and administer psychological tests to individuals to determine their risk of suicide and the dangers they pose to others. Testing may include the Violence Risk Appraisal Guide (Harris, Rice, & Quinsey, 1993), Violence Prediction Scheme (Webster, Harris, Rice, Cormier, & Quinsey, 1994), or other measures designed to determine the probability that an individual will engage in violent behavior.

Psychological damages. Civil court cases often involve plaintiffs who seek compensation for psychological injuries caused by a second party, including emotional distress, posttraumatic stress disorder, and depression. For example, consider a parent who has witnessed the death of a child due to negligence on the part of an individual or company (e.g., an amusement ride accident caused by lack of regular maintenance). The parent may sue the individual or company to provide financial compensation for the emotional and psychological trauma that he or she has experienced. Forensic psychologists play a critical role in evaluating emotional and psychological trauma in such cases.

Forensic psychologists also provide evaluations within the context of workers' compensation cases. Workers who suffer serious physical injuries that leave them with chronic pain often demonstrate psychological symptoms such as anxiety and depression. A forensic psychologist might assess a plaintiff in a workers' compensation case to determine whether he or she has sustained emotional or psychological trauma.

In each of these cases, the task of a forensic psychologist is to evaluate the psychological state of the individual in question by conducting interviews and administering psychological tests to determine whether the injuries are veracious, the result of exaggeration, stress, or malingering.

Psychological autopsy. Sometimes a forensic psychologist is asked to conduct a psychological autopsy—that is, provide an evaluation of the deceased person's state of mind before death (Shneidman, 1994). Such an evaluation may be requested when a life insurance company suspects that an accidental death is instead a suicide (and therefore not subject to death benefits). A psychological autopsy may also be conducted to evaluate the individual's capacity to create or modify a will before death, or to determine whether a death is a homicide, suicide, or accident. Clearly, psychological autopsies are unusual and challenging evaluations. Typically the forensic psychologist will examine the individual's past medical, occupational, and mental health records, as well as conduct interviews with persons who knew the deceased. Conclusions from a psychological autopsy often cannot be stated with certainty (Shneidman, 1994) and the overall validity of psychological autopsies has been questioned (Selkin, 1994).

As you can see, forensic psychologists engage in a wide range of assessment and evaluation activities within the context of criminal and civil court cases. Many forensic psychologists work in private practice, and some criminal forensic psychologists work in state institutions, such as secure forensic units, community mental health centers, and hospitals, where they conduct risk assessments of offenders and other at-risk individuals before they are released (Kuther & Morgan, 2004).

ADVANTAGES AND DISADVANTAGES OF A CAREER IN FORENSIC EVALUATION

The primary advantages of forensic evaluation work are the job satisfaction that most evaluators experience as well as the potential to earn an income that may range from comfortable to lucrative. Entry-level psychologists providing forensic services in hospitals and community settings may begin at approximately $43,000 annually, but salaries tend to vary by state and jurisdiction (American Psychology-Law Society, 1998). Forensic psychologists in private practice typically bill between $150 and $250 per hour, but must work hard at making a steady income. It is difficult to predict ups and downs in a private practice, so financial planning and marketing or promotion of one's services is essential.

An important disadvantage of a career in forensic evaluation is the potential for lawsuits and ethics complaints filed against forensic examiners. Those who specialize in child custody and child abuse cases are especially likely to experience board complaints and ethics charges. For example, it has been estimated that 7–10% of ethics complaints reported to the American Psychological Association are against child custody evaluators (Glassman, 1998). Fortunately, frivolous cases often are dismissed quickly; only 1% of psychologists charged with ethics complaints receive disciplinary action (Kirkland & Kirkland, 2001). However, even frivolous lawsuits or ethics complaints can be costly in terms of finances, time, stress, and professional image. And finally, forensic examiners may experience considerable stress because many court cases are highly emotional for all parties (e.g., child custody cases).

Although forensic psychologists often write forensic evaluations that inform the court, sometimes they are asked to supplement their reports with testimony. The opportunity to provide courtroom testimony may be an advantage or disadvantage to a career in forensic evaluation, depending on your education, experience, and taste for the confrontative nature of legal challenges (Hess, 1998; Lloyd-Bostock, 1988). The cross-examination may challenge your education, training, competence, and the validity and reliability of forensic assessment. To learn more about the challenges and rewards of providing expert testimony, see Chapter 4.

TRAINING TIPS FOR CAREERS IN FORENSIC PSYCHOLOGY

Students who seek careers in forensic psychology should seek a doctoral degree in forensic psychology, or clinical or counseling psychology, followed by a predoctoral or postdoctoral internship (i.e., field experience) in forensic psychology, specializing in forensic assessments (see Chapter 6 for more information about graduate programs in forensic psychology). A solid understanding of pathology, clinical assessment, and treatment, experience with both criminal and noncriminal clients, and an understanding of social and cultural norms and issues, is essential background for conducting forensic evaluations. You'll need to understand theory and scientific methodology (e.g., knowledge of scientific validity issues, research design, statistics, and testing) in order to explain the validity of your assessments in a report or oral presentation.

In addition to a doctoral degree and experience in forensic settings, psychologists who wish to provide forensic evaluations must seek licensure. To obtain a license to practice, you must complete: (1) a doctoral program in psychology; (2) 2 years of supervised experience (with 1 year postdoctoral supervision); (3) a multiple-choice national examination covering a broad range of issues relevant to the practice of psychology; (4) a written jurisprudence examination that assesses knowledge about the specific ethical code and practice-related laws of each state; and sometimes (5) an oral examination, varying by state (Kuther & Morgan, 2004). Courses in law with the opportunity to read legal cases and observe legal proceedings will help to familiarize you with the legal aspects of forensic psychology. Finally, seek a mentor: a senior colleague with forensic experience to whom you can turn for advice.

SUGGESTED READINGS

Ackerman, M. J. (1999). *Essentials of forensic psychological assessment.* New York: Wiley.

Grisso, T. (1998). *Forensic evaluation of juveniles.* Sarasota, FL: Professional Resource Exchange.

Hess, A. K., & Weiner, I. B. (1999). *The handbook of forensic psychology.* New York: Wiley.

Huss, M. T. (2001). Psychology and law, now and in the next century: The promise of an emerging area of psychology. In J. S. Halonen & S. F. Davis (Eds.), *The many faces of psychological research in the 21st century.* Society for the Teaching of Psychology. Retrieved on June, 18, 2003, at
http://teachpsych.lemoyne.edu/teachpsych/faces/text/Ch11.htm.

Melton, G. B., Petrila, J., Poythress, N. G., & Slobogin, C. (1997). *Psychological evaluations for the courts: A handbook for mental health professionals and lawyers* (2nd ed.). New York: Guilford.

WEB RESOURCES

Juvenile Forensic Evaluation Resource Center
http://www.ilppp.virginia.edu/Research_Projects/juvenile_forensic_evaluation_r.html

Forensic Psychology Services
http://www.psychologyinfo.com/forensic/

Forensic Psychology Database
http://flash.lakeheadu.ca/~pals/forensics/

American Board of Forensic Psychology
http://www.abfp.com/

David Willshire's Forensic Psychology & Psychiatry Links
http://members.optushome.com.au/dwillsh/

National Criminal Justice Reference Service
http://www.ncjrs.org/

PROFILE 2.1: KAREN FRANKLIN, PH.D.

Karen Franklin earned her doctorate in clinical psychology at the California School of Professional Psychology. She is licensed in the states of California and Washington, and has completed a postdoctoral fellowship in forensic psychology at the University of Washington. She is a widely recognized expert on the psychosocial motivations of hate crime offenders. Her research on this topic has garnered the Monette/Horwitz Trust Award (2001) and a Harry Frank Guggenheim Fellowship (1996). Her peer-reviewed publications have appeared in the American Behavioral Scientist, Journal of Interpersonal Violence, Encyclopedia of Violence, Encyclopedia of Criminology, and Journal of Forensic Psychology Practice, among others. Currently, she has an independent forensic practice in the San Francisco Bay Area, specializing in the evaluation of adult offenders. She also teaches forensic psychology at the California School of Professional Psychology. Dr. Franklin provided me with the details of her work and suggestions for her students.

Forensic psychology is not my first career, nor even my second. I previously worked as a typesetter, a newspaper reporter, a private investigator, and even a tobacco barner. Of all of my careers, forensic psychology is the ideal one for someone with a low threshold for boredom.

I became interested in forensic psychology while working as a criminal investigator. I was putting together "mitigating evidence" for defendants facing capital murder trials. Working on a team with experts and attorneys, I observed that forensic psychologists got paid good money to do what I liked best—study what makes people tick.

My undergraduate education in journalism and my career as an investigator armed me with two tools essential to the forensic psychologist—writing skills and detective skills. After obtaining a Ph.D. in clinical psychology, I pursued advanced training in forensic psychology through a postdoctoral fellowship. To further hone my skills in preparation for independent practice, I also worked briefly at two prisons and a mental hospital.

My forensic practice focuses on adult criminal cases. In a typical week, I might conduct evaluations at several jails, consult with attorneys, review research on various topics, and write reports of my findings. The issues I tackle are varied. The bread-and-butter work is evaluating defendants' competency to stand trial. Other frequent issues include a defendant's mental state at the time of an offense or a person's risk of future violence or sexual offending. At other times, I am involved as a "pure expert," that is, someone who discusses the empirical literature on a topic without evaluating any of the parties in a case.

Like many forensic psychologists, I stay active in academic and re-search pursuits as well. I teach forensic psychology to graduate students, review articles for publication in journals, and occasionally write an article in my research area. Fortuitously, my dissertation topic—the motivations of hate crime offenders—garnered a lot of interest at the time, and I earned some prominence in that niche. This has some overlay with my clinical practice, in that I may be called on to evaluate a defendant if anti-gay bias is a suspected element.

As compared with general clinical psychology, forensic work has distinct advantages and disadvantages. On the plus side, the work is fascinating, and it provides enormous variety. I have a great deal of independence, and some ability to pick and choose the work. Forensic psychologists are also accorded quite a bit of respect in the legal arena.

At the same time, the work is hard, and requires rigorous attention to detail. The practitioner must stay up to date on the latest developments in numerous areas. She must be skilled at psychological testing. Under adversarial scrutiny, a mistake can be costly, leading to public embarrassment or worse. Excellent writing skills are essential, as we write numerous and lengthy reports and our written presentation can make or break our reputation. Forensic psychologists must also develop the business acumen and thick skin necessary to deal with attorneys and other clients who may have agendas that conflict with our values, ethics, or practical interests.

At the present time, there is no single acceptable training model for forensic psychologists. Students interested in pursuing a career in forensic psychology should get a firm undergraduate and graduate foundation in the science of psychology (including issues of research design, statistics, and testing). Then, select one or more career niches, and take courses relevant to these. For example, if you intend to do child custody work, you should become an expert on child development. If you intend to work with juvenile offenders, pursue an internship in an adolescent setting. Become especially knowledgeable about cultural and social influences on behavior. Some course work on legal theory is also advantageous. The dissertation has a potential to open doors, so the topic should be carefully chosen. It should be something that not only fascinates you, but also has potential marketability. (Hint: Do not study the mind of the serial killer!)

After obtaining a doctoral degree in clinical psychology, I recommend pursuing a formal postgraduate fellowship through which you can get the advanced training, experience, and mentoring necessary to launch a successful career. Ideally, this should be in the geographic locale and among the population with whom you intend to work. I also recommend working in a forensic hospital or correctional setting during your training or early career. Stay in these settings only long enough to become familiar with their workings, and not so long that your values become corrupted by them.

PROFILE 2.2: EVAN NELSON, PH.D.

Dr. Evan Nelson is a Licensed Clinical Psychologist and a Certified Sex Offender Treatment Provider in the Commonwealth of Virginia. He holds a Diplomate in Forensic Psychology from the American Board of Professional Psychology (ABPP). He earned his Ph.D. in clinical psychology from the University of North Carolina at Chapel Hill, completed an internship at the Indiana University School of Medicine, and performed his postdoctoral residency at the Forensic Unit of Central State Hospital in Petersburg, Virginia. Dr. Nelson has been an expert in thousands of criminal cases including more than 150 capital murder trials, and his work has been cited in 18 Virginia Appellate and Supreme Court decisions as well as in the recent U.S. Supreme Court decision on Atkins v. Commonwealth.

Dr. Nelson provided responses to several questions I posed concerning his background and assessment of the field of forensic psychology.

How did you become interested in forensic psychology?

The fact that my career is in forensic psychology had more to do with opportunity knocking than with any preplanning. In graduate school, I trained as a generalist in clinical psychology, with the hope of practicing marital and family therapy as a specialty. However, after my internship I needed to get a job in Richmond, Virginia, because that was where my wife's psychology internship was going to be—and a position at Virginia's flagship forensic inpatient was the best employment I could find at the time. There were no good positions in marital and family therapy for an entry-level doctor when I needed a job, and hence I became a forensic specialist.

In retrospect I consider myself lucky that I fell into the forensic hospital job. It turned out that I liked working with patients with more severe psychopathology, enjoyed the detective-like work of conducting a forensic evaluation, and loved the intense experience of testifying at a trial. Seeing a crime through the eyes of a mentally ill defendant is an extraordinary way to come to understand the power of the mind and its influence on behavior. Working in a forensic hospital provided in-depth training and a wealth of professional contacts that made it easy to transition to private practice after 3 years of experience.

What are your specialties and areas of expertise?

The bulk of my practice is evaluations of criminal defendants to see if they are competent to stand trial, legally insane at the time of the alleged offense, and to assess issues related to sentencing. I have special expertise in the areas of capital sentencing (death penalty hearings) and sex offender risk assessment. In addition to criminal evaluations, I also evaluate persons applying for disability and fathers engaged in custody battles who have been accused of sexual improprieties.

A typical day involves traveling to a jail or prison, interviewing and testing a defendant, reviewing the offense and treatment records related to the case, contacting witnesses to the crime or family members of the defendant to learn their perspectives on what happened and the defendant's mental health history, consulting with the lawyers, and then writing a report. In about one of 20 cases, I testify about my results.

What trends do you see for forensic psychology?

It is my opinion that forensic psychology will grow while many other sectors of psychology will shrink. The world is becoming more litigious, society is becoming more conservative and therefore prosecuting more cases, and the failing economy after 9/11/01 will mean a rise in crime over the next few years—all of which creates opportunities for forensic specialists. The high visibility of forensic psychology via Court TV, television shows such as CSI and Profiler, and criminal cases of national interest (e.g., Andrea Yates's insanity plea in Texas, questions about the competency of Zacarias Moussaoui to plead guilty to conspiracy to commit acts of terrorism) has already led to increased interest in the field.

In addition, the psycholegal arena is one of the few domains left where a doctorate degree is a requisite credential and where persons with advanced degrees are compensated for their special expertise. I predict that psychologists in general clinical practice will increasingly diversify their practices to include forensics because they can be paid well and have professional prestige; I never have to haggle with an insurance company, as do mainstream therapists.

The field of forensic psychology is also likely to become more data focused. In the past 10 years, the complexity of psychological tests has increased and the legal system is demanding that experts provide more proof for the validity of their procedures (see Daubert v. Merrell Dow Pharmaceuticals). With the advent of high speed Internet connections, some aspects of forensic psychology will probably transition to videophone consultations, somewhat like telemedicine.

What advantages/disadvantages do you see to becoming a forensic psychologist?

As noted previously, in my opinion there is more job security in forensics than in being a general therapist because of the economics of the changing marketplace for psychology. On average, forensic psychologists earn more money than their counterparts whose practices focus on non-forensic therapy. The work itself is very exciting in large part because of the nature of criminal cases, but also because being an expert means one is an important part of the legal process and in a unique position to educate lawyers, judges, and juries about mental health and mental illness.

On the other hand, this is a stressful business. The successful forensic expert needs a veneer of cynicism and a thick skin to survive. This field involves working closely with criminals who have done heinous deeds, coping with the raw emotions of victims as well as the family members of the defendants, and even life-and-death matters such as in a death penalty hearing. One has to be able to stay emotionally detached from the details of the case. Being an expert can be bruising on the ego, too: testimony can be brutal and attorneys and the media often comment on an expert's credibility or personality without any opportunity for the psychologist to respond.

The pace of the job is very rapid: courts and lawyers demand a rapid response from experts, even though legal proceedings themselves make take months or years to reach a conclusion. Thus, being able to tolerate stress and constant change are critical elements in the practice of forensics. Frequently, forensic experts must travel to perform evaluations outside of their vicinity and this can be a strain on family life.

CORRECTIONAL AND POLICE PSYCHOLOGY

CHAPTER GUIDE

When we consider psychologists' involvement in the criminal justice system, we tend to focus on the psychologist who provides forensic evaluations or expert testimony for criminal and civil court cases. We usually forget psychologists in prison or correctional settings and others in law enforcement or police settings. This chapter explores the activities of correctional and police psychologists, often neglected members of the mental health community. We'll examine the scope, as well as advantages and disadvantages to careers in correctional and police psychology.

CORRECTIONAL PSYCHOLOGY

The U.S. prison population has risen to a record-breaking 2 million inmates (Boothby & Clements, 2002). Given the varied mental health needs of inmates, correctional careers are becoming more popular choices for psychologists with forensic interests (Murray, 1998). Over 2,000 psychologists are currently employed by correctional institutions (Boothby & Clements, 2002), yet most people, psychologists and students alike, know little about this career option.

Scope of the Discipline

The mission of the psychologist within a correctional setting is "to assist in the rehabilitation of offenders and in their reintegration into society" (Hawk, 1997, p. 335). Psychologists who work in correctional settings engage in direct service delivery by conducting psychological assessments as inmates enter the prison system, diagnosing and treating mental disorders, and providing basic mental health services to inmates (Boothby & Clements, 2000). A large part of their work entails preventing mental disorders that may develop in response to the deprivation and stress that inmates experience within the prison environment (Milan, Chin, & Nguyen, 1999). Crisis management is an essential activity of psychologists within correctional settings. An inmate may go into crisis after disciplinary action, failure to get parole, or threats by other inmates; many inmates exhibit prolonged crises resulting from overall adjustment problems (Mobley, 1999).

In addition to individual therapy, correctional psychologists develop and evaluate group therapy and rehabilitation programs to address substance abuse and other addictions, sex offending, suicide ideation, anger management, parenting skills, stress management, and coping with the difficult transition back to the community (as a way of preventing recidivism) (Hawk, 1997; Morgan, Winterowd, & Ferrell, 1999). Correctional psychologists also play a role in probation and parole decisions by conducting risk assessments to predict the likelihood of future antisocial conduct by an offender (Heilbrun, 1999). A risk assessment entails examining the offender's social and criminal history, prison file, results from psychological tests, and interviews to assess the danger that an individual poses to society (Heilbrun, 1999).

Correctional psychologists promote mental health within the correctional setting, which includes addressing the mental health needs of staff and family members during and after prison disturbances, hostage situations, and other traumatic events (Hawk, 1997). They train staff in confrontation avoidance, anger management, coping skills, stress management, and methods for surviving hostage situations. Correctional psychologists also engage in research to improve the quality of psychological services offered within correctional settings (Milan et al., 1999).

Advantages and Disadvantages of a Career in Correctional Psychology

Correctional mental health professionals report high levels of job satisfaction (Boothby & Clements, 2000; Ferrell, Morgan, & Winterowd, 2000); however, correctional environments are stressful (Brodsky, 1982). Psychologists may find themselves in multiple and sometimes competing roles, including both treatment and control. Correctional psychologists may find themselves performing correctional officer duties such as searching inmate cells for contraband and patrolling (Boothby & Clements, 2002). Employees of correctional institutions often are required to obtain additional training in self-defense, firearms, or other security measures (Boothby & Clements, 2002). The varied duties of a correctional psychologist may be an advantage or disadvantage, depending on individual tastes, strengths, and weaknesses.

A disadvantage to a career in correctional psychology is that there are generally few opportunities for advancement outside of prison administration (Boothby & Clements, 2002). Correctional psychologists also have very large caseloads and are responsible for hundreds of inmates. The overload of work can lead to burnout. However, the clients are diverse, which can be challenging and exciting. A psychologist in corrections will work with a wide variety of clients imprisoned for diverse crimes including robbery, homicide, rape, embezzlement, child molestation, drunk driving, and many more. Clients often differ in background, experiences, and world-views. Meeting the needs of a large and diverse caseload can be demanding, but also gratifying. Often the only thing that clients have in common is incarceration.

Given the rise in the prison population, correctional psychology offers job security, as well as a comfortable salary. In the Federal Bureau of Prisons, the starting annual salary for doctoral-level psychologists is approximately $42,000, with an average salary of $61,800 (Kuther & Morgan, 2004; Boothby & Clements, 2000). State correctional facilities offer an average salary of $53,400 for doctoral-level providers (Boothby & Clements, 2000). In addition, there are many opportunities for master's-level practitioners within correctional facilities, and salaries for master's-level practitioners are higher in corrections than in other areas of practice. For example, the median salary for a master's-level clinician in 1996 was approximately $27,000 annually (Auguste, Wicherski, & Kohout, 1999; adjusted to $31,300 in 2002 with a 3% annual adjustment), but $40,100 in corrections (Boothby & Clements, 2000).

Training Tips for a Career in Correctional Psychology

A doctoral degree in clinical or counseling psychology provides the necessary training in psychological assessment and treatment to secure employment in a correctional facility. If you're interested in a career in correctional psychology, take additional graduate courses in the assessment and treatment of personality disorders, forensic psychology, criminal justice or law, detection of malingering (i.e., faking), crisis intervention, and substance abuse evaluation and treatment (Boothby & Clements, 2000). Practicum experience working with offenders or other difficult clients (e.g., clients mandated to attend treatment, psychiatric inpatients) will strengthen your application for employment at correctional institutions (Boothby & Clements, 2000; Kuther & Morgan, 2004). Also consider pursuing internship or postdoctoral experiences in correctional settings or secure forensic institutions. At present, nine accredited doctoral-level internship sites are available through the Federal Bureau of Prisons (Kuther & Morgan, 2004). For more information about graduate training, see Chapter 6.

POLICE PSYCHOLOGY

Police psychology has become increasingly prominent in law enforcement (Delprino & Bahn, 1988) despite law enforcement officers' sometimes wariness about psychological services (Max, 2000). Police psychologists may be independently practicing consultants to law enforcement agencies or may be employed by law enforcement agencies (sometimes sworn in as law enforcement officers) (Bartol, 1996).

Scope of the Discipline

Police psychologists provide a variety of evaluative, counseling, training, and support services to police agencies including the following (Scrivner & Kurke, 1995):

- **Selection of police officers.** One of the most common activities of police psychologists is to provide preemployment evaluations (Super, 1999).

Police work is very stressful and requires individuals who are psychologically healthy and prepared for the many challenges entailed in law enforcement. Police psychologists evaluate applicants to rule out those who lack the disposition and personality style to cope with stress that a law enforcement career requires.

- **Training of police officers.** Police psychologists train officers to enhance their human relations skills, including how to be sensitive to victims' needs and understand the nature of, and appropriate response to, domestic violence. Other areas of psychological training that police psychologists provide include hostage negotiation, policies for reducing police brutality, and strategies for dealing with terrorists.
- **Fitness for duty and special unit evaluations.** Critical incidents, such as the death of a partner or injury in the line of duty, can cause tremendous stress. Police psychologists evaluate officers who have been exposed to critical incidents to determine their ability to cope and return to duty. Police psychologists also conduct assessments to assist with promotional decisions for specialized police assignments such as Special Weapons and Tactics (SWAT), Tactical Response Teams (TRT), and Hostage Negotiation Teams (HNT).
- **Counseling.** Stress is a prevalent problem in law enforcement (Anson & Bloom, 1988). Police psychologists provide counseling services to help officers and their families cope with the stressful lifestyle.
- **Operational support.** Police psychologists provide officers with field consultation (e.g., assisting in the apprehension or security of a mentally ill person, or determining whether a death occurred by homicide or suicide), hostage negotiations, and, less frequently, investigative activities (Bartol, 1996). They also communicate the relevant current research (e.g., influences on the accuracy of eyewitnesses or identification through police lineups, and how interrogative suggestibility may influence a suspect) to police in order to increase the effectiveness of investigations.
- **Organizational development and support.** Police psychologists assist management with administrative decision making, team building, and organizational development.

Police psychology encompasses a broad range of activities, but not all police psychologists engage in each of these activities. Police psychologists tend to spend most of their time in counseling, and in the screening and selection of law enforcement officers (Bartol, 1996; Bergen, Aceto, & Chadziewicz, 1992).

Advantages and Disadvantages of a Career in Police Psychology

A career in police psychology offers opportunities to help law enforcement officers deal with the stresses of their jobs, and to help the community at large.

Although police psychologists might experience mistrust on the part of officers (Wrightsman, 2001), research suggests that most police psychologists perceive little animosity from officers (Bergen et al., 1992). Perhaps the largest disadvantage to this career, like careers in correctional psychology, is stress. Police departments are very busy and demanding places. Often police psychologists are asked to help with a variety of tasks, which is exciting and interesting, but also taxing. Many police psychologists feel as if they are asked to be all things to all people and sometimes are asked to work in areas that are beyond their expertise or competence (Super, 1999). Needless to say, balancing multiple duties can be taxing; the high levels of stress that police psychologists experience can lead to burn out.

Although it is a demanding profession, police psychologists report very high levels of job satisfaction (Bergen et al., 1992). Entry-level salaries for police psychologists are commensurate with other entry-level doctoral psychology positions with an average annual salary in the low $40,000s (Kuther & Morgan , 2004). One survey of in-house police psychologists, with an average experience of 11.8 years (SD = 4.8 years), found that they earned a median annual salary of $53,000 (Bartol, 1996). Finally, police psychology is a growth field. Surveys of police psychologists show that they perceive the current and future job market as very good, with excellent opportunities for expansion (Bartol, 1996).

Training Tips for a Career in Police Psychology

Similar to correctional psychology, most police psychologists are trained as clinical or counseling psychologists (Kuther & Morgan, 2004). There are very few formal opportunities for training in police psychology during graduate school. If you're interested in a career as a police psychologist, clinical skills in assessment, diagnosis, treatment, and crisis intervention are essential (Bartol, 1996). Supplement your clinical and counseling knowledge with courses in psychology and law to understand the legal issues that influence clinical practice within the criminal justice system. An understanding of job analysis procedures, team building, and leadership from courses in industrial and organizational psychology will serve you well (Bartol, 1996). A background in statistics and research methodology will round out your background and provide the necessary expertise to evaluate programs and initiatives within police departments. Finally, seek predoctoral and postdoctoral internships or practica experience in police or criminal justice settings in order to obtain practical (and very valuable) experience in police psychology.

SUGGESTED READINGS

Bartol, C. R. (1996). Police psychology then, now, and beyond. *Criminal Justice and Behavior, 23,* 70–89.

Blau, T. H. (1994). *Psychological services for law enforcement.* New York: Wiley.

Boothby, J. L., & Clements, C. B. (2000). A national survey of correctional psychologists. *Criminal Justice & Behavior, 27*(6), 716–732.

Hawk, K. M. (1997). Personal reflections on a career in correctional psychology. *Professional Psychology: Research & Practice, 28*(4), 335–337.

Flanagan, C. L. (1995). Legal issues regarding police psychology. In M. I. Kurke & E. M. Scrivner (Eds.), *Police psychology into the 21st century* (pp. 93–107). Hillsdale, NJ: Erlbaum.

Kurke, M. I., & Scrivner, E. M. (1995). *Police psychology into the 21st century.* Hillsdale, NJ: Erlbaum.

Super, J. T. (1999). Forensic psychology and law enforcement. In A. K. Hess, & I. B. Weiner (Eds.), *The handbook of forensic psychology* (pp. 409–439). New York: Wiley.

WEB RESOURCES

The Society for Police and Criminal Psychology
http://cep.jmu.edu/spcp/

The Career Path Less Traveled
http://www.apa.org/monitor/feb01/careerpath.html"

Prison and Probation Services Psychology
http://www.hmprisonservice.gov.uk/corporate/dynpage.asp?Page=229

International Association of Chiefs of Police
http://www.theiacp.org/div_sec_com/sections/Psych_Srvcs/fitness.htm

Corrections Connection
http://www.corrections.com/

National Criminal Justice Reference Service
http://www.ncjrs.org/

National Institute of Corrections
http://www.nicic.org/

American Association for Correctional Psychology
http://www.eaacp.org/cgi-bin/index.pl

Police Psychology Online
http://www.policepsych.com/

Heavy Badge
http://www.heavybadge.com/

PROFILE 3.1 : TERRENCE W. DeMAY, ED.D.

The first U.S. casualty of the war on terrorism in Afghanistan was a Central Intelligence Agency (CIA) officer. Johnny Michael "Mike" Spann was killed Nov. 25 during an uprising of Taliban prisoners. Within 24 hours of his death, CIA psychologists offered support to all those who needed help in coping with the tragedy, from his family to his coworkers, domestically and overseas.

That's just one example of the many critical roles CIA psychologists play in support of America's national security. In an interview with the Monitor, psychologist Terrence W. DeMay, Ed.D., offers a glimpse of the important work of Agency psychologists. DeMay is chief of the Mental Health Division, Office of Medical Services, at the CIA.

What is the psychologist's role at the CIA?

One of our primary roles is to help CIA employees with the unique challenges they are required to cope with: security requirements, intense training, unconventional tasking, unfamiliar working conditions, unexpected and time sensitive challenges, multiple and competing requirements, and the burden of a secretive, silent and sometimes misunderstood mission.

CIA employees and their families find themselves living in unfamiliar, unpredictable, unfriendly, unhealthy, or potentially dangerous surroundings. Some are asked to endure hardships and inconveniences never experienced by most people. Some are placed directly in harm's way in service of their country, living and working in areas of the world affected by natural disasters, manmade disasters, crime, terrorism, and war.

They are not asked to take on these challenges alone. Within the CIA, Office of Medical Services (OMS) psychologists, psychiatrists and other support personnel care for their mental and physical well-being from the onset of employment. The Mental Health Division of OMS develops and implements worldwide response capabilities that address both the needs of the individual and unique organizational requirements. The work of CIA psychologists is grounded firmly in traditional clinical psychology and accepted professional practices. Screening, evaluation, selection, consultation, crisis intervention, short-term counseling, follow-up, and training are the cornerstones of a program that enjoys widespread acceptance and has experienced consistent growth during the last decade.

Screening potential employees must also be an important part of your job.

Psychologists evaluate all candidates for CIA employment to determine their suitability for a position of trust. Pre-employment evaluations focus on clinical disorders, risk factors, and vulnerabilities that might impact adversely on the ability of the individual to protect classified information. Reliability, responsibility, impulse control, and good judgment are required of all employees. We use structured interviews, developmental histories, psychological testing, and collateral data to determine suitability for employment. We make recommendations in the context of a broader applicant-processing system that includes input from security professionals, human resources specialists and substantive experts.

Some candidates for unusually sensitive positions—those requiring labor-intensive or expensive training, or positions involving safety issues—complete additional psychological testing and interviews. We conduct job analyses to determine the specific requirements of each position. These analyses are updated on the basis of changing requirements and manager, trainer, and incumbent input.

CIA psychologists also participate directly in many training activities that enhance their first-hand knowledge of Agency requirements. We develop testing and interview protocols to address the strengths and weaknesses of each candidate in relationship to the current requirements of the anticipated position.

How do most employees fare under what can be challenging work environments?

Our pre-employment screening and evaluation appear to contribute to a relatively healthy and resilient work force capable of supporting the Agency's unique mission. Base rates of diagnosable mental health problems are significantly lower for Agency employees than they are for comparable age groups in the general population. Agency employees also tend to experience fewer severe or disabling conditions and fewer life-threatening conditions. Rates of relapse are lower than what would usually be expected.

Agency employees are not immune to psychological disorders, however, and in some cases are at greater-than-average risk because of the unique stressors they are asked to endure routinely. CIA psychologists attempt to understand the potential impact of these stressors, develop relevant preventive interventions, monitor individual and systemic impact, and ensure the availability of consultation, treatment and follow-up. Thousands of employees also attend mental health workshops, seminars, and briefings conducted by Agency psychologists each year. Coping with conflict, coping with organizational change, time management and stress management are just a few of the topics covered in these popular presentations.

Do psychologists play a role in the assignment of employees and their families overseas?

CIA psychologists and psychiatrists screen employees and their families. We consider the needs of the individuals involved in the context of the demands of the anticipated assignment, support and resources available, and types of problems encountered in the past. We interview employees and sometimes their spouses and review the developmental histories of their children, and pay particular attention to their psychoeducational needs. We seek second opinions from specialists when doubts regarding assignability remain. Candidates for particularly unpleasant, inconvenient, or dangerous assignments receive additional attention from CIA psychologists who are knowledgeable about the living and working conditions they will encounter. These individuals participate in additional interviews and complete additional psychological testing. Psychologists are often asked to participate in multidisciplinary assignment panels to assist management in making informed decisions that can affect the career of the individual and the Agency's mission.

What happens when a CIA employee needs psychological services?

Psychological problems that occur in the context of an overseas assignment can be disruptive and costly. The success of CIA personnel is determined at least in part by their ability to maintain a low profile and function with relative anonymity. Employees in distress can draw unwanted attention to themselves and to their parent organization.

In the worst-case scenario, untreated problems can result in the exposure of clandestine activities and possibly even the loss of life. In the best-case scenario, mission-critical activities are unaffected but the individual must be returned home for appropriate treatment that often is not available overseas. Bringing an employee home can result in lost productivity, disruption of spousal employment, disruption of the education of children, and a significant financial burden for the individual and the organization.

CIA psychologists are prepared to assist in the prevention and remediation of mental health problems wherever they occur. They travel extensively, providing routine consultations and responding to crises. Although travel in some parts of the world is difficult, CIA psychologists and psychiatrists can generally get to any employee in less than 24 hours. Pre-employment screening, pre-assignment screening, and rapid response capabilities combine to minimize the number of employees and family members that must be returned home short of tour for mental health reasons.

Do you feel that your role is well integrated into the Agency's overall goals?

The success and professional effectiveness of CIA psychologists depend on their ability to understand individual needs in the context of the unique mission they support. Throughout their careers, they participate in the same kind of specialized training afforded employees outside of the mental health arena—experiencing the same stressors, enduring the same long hours and developing some of the same knowledge, skills, and abilities. Understanding of organizational dynamics is fostered through participation on interdisciplinary panels that focus on recruitment, hiring, training, risk management, and emergency response readiness.

Psychologists have become welcome partners in a wide range of forums impacting on both the individual and the Agency. Some components within the Agency have psychologists assigned to their area of responsibility on a full-time basis, giving them immediate and ongoing access to a behavioral scientist who becomes intimately familiar with their requirements.

Are you able to engage with psychology colleagues outside the Agency?

Yes. There is a great deal of emphasis on multidisciplinary service delivery and on the continuing education needed to sustain and enhance clinical competencies. CIA psychologists work closely with staff psychiatrists, staff physicians and other medical specialists. Continuing education needs are surveyed yearly and outside speakers with substantive expertise are invited to share their knowledge. Psychologists from other government organizations with similar missions are often invited to attend, creating additional opportunities for professional interactions and development. Agency psychologists also attend continuing education programs sponsored by other organizations.

In addition, Agency psychologists are encouraged to participate in other professional activities that encourage interactions and exchanges of ideas with their non-Agency peers. Some have part-time private practices in the evenings that broaden their perspective on current practice issues.

What do you like best about your job at the CIA?

The challenges of providing mental health services within the intelligence community are many and varied—but so are the rewards. When earthquakes erupt, planes crash, assaults occur, buildings are bombed, or people are wounded or killed by acts of war, CIA psychologists are there to minimize the impact of the traumatic event, formulate appropriate intervention strategies, and coordinate follow-up plans. When a Headquarters employee seeks help for clinical symptoms, problems related to job satisfaction, or more common problems of daily living, CIA psychologists are there to assess the nature and extent of the problem and facilitate its resolution. And when the impact of a traumatic event, clinical disorder or situational stressor extends beyond the affected employee, support is available for spouses, children, and other family members.

Thousands of miles from home or across the hallway at CIA Headquarters, CIA psychologists address the mental health needs of all employees.

(from Monitor on Psychology, 33 (4), April, 2002.) Copyright © 2002 by the American Psychological Association. Reprinted with permission.

CONSULTING

CHAPTER GUIDE

With over 18 million new lawsuits each year (Myers & Arena, 2001), court-related activities have emerged as an important area of work for psychologists. In this chapter we'll explore three roles that psychologists play within the legal system: trial consultants, mediators, and expert witnesses.

TRIAL CONSULTANT

Trial consulting is a growing field and one in which psychologists are uniquely suited, given their ability to analyze and understand human behavior (Myers & Arena, 2001). It has been estimated that there are about 700 independent trial consultants and 400 trial consulting firms within the United States (Streier, 1999; Wrightsman, 2001).

Scope of the Discipline

Trial consultants (also known as a litigation consultants or jury consultants) assist attorneys in preparing for, and carrying out, trials. They assess the general public's perceptions, knowledge, and biases about a given case, provide advice about jury selection, trial strategy, and presentation, and assist lawyers in preparing witnesses for examination during the trial.

Community surveys and focus groups. Trial consultants conduct surveys and focus groups with community members for at least two purposes: "trial by survey" and support for change of venue requests (Nietzel & Dillehay, 1986). Trial by survey entails surveying (through written questionnaires, interviews, and focus groups) a sample of community members to identify the major issues in a case and gain the perspectives of individuals from the same community as the jurors. Attorneys might test litigation tactics and presentation techniques and gather the respondents' reactions to determine how to present the evidence in the most favorable light.

Community surveys can also be used to determine whether a change in venue is warranted. Research has shown that pretrial publicity can bias potential jurors (Studebaker & Penrod, 1997). Trial consultants assess the impact of pretrial publicity by conducting surveys to determine the extent of the public's familiarity with and opinions about the case. Once the survey is completed, the trial consultant examines the results and prepares a report explaining the methodology, findings, and conclusions regarding the extent to which a defendant can expect an unbiased jury (Wrightsman, 2001). If a large proportion of community members are familiar with the case and if those who are familiar with the case tend to believe that the defendant is guilty, a change of venue is warranted (Myers & Arena, 2001).

If the attorney decides to move forward with a motion for change of venue (a request to move the trial to a community that has been exposed to less publicity about the case), the trial consultant will prepare an affidavit for the court that explains the literature regarding the effects of pretrial publicity on juror bias, the survey methodology, and his or her conclusions. The judge will then schedule a preliminary hearing in which the trial consultant testifies about the survey and his or her recommendations (Wrightsman, 2001).

Jury selection. We are most familiar with the trial consultant's role in jury selection, given the publicity afforded jury selection in recent high-profile cases (e.g., the O.J. Simpson trial). Trial consultants provide attorneys with advice on the demographic and attitudinal characteristics of individuals who take a favorable position on the case. They present individuals from the community with information about the case; they then measure the individuals' responses, as well as demographic and attitudinal characteristics to develop a profile of the "ideal juror," or juror who is likely to side with the attorney's desired verdict. Under some circumstances, trial consultants may also use measures to screen prospective jurors for biases, such as The Revised Legal Attitudes Questionnaire (Kravitz, Cutler, & Brock, 1993) or The Juror Bias Scale (Kassin & Wrightsman, 1983), as well as general attitudinal traits that may be relevant to a given civil case, such as attitudes about risk taking, the "litigation explosion" (the increase in lawsuits within recent years), or attitudes about personal responsibility and corporate responsibility (Wrightsman, 2001).

Witness preparation. Many witnesses are not as effective as they can be. The trial consultant's role in witness preparation is not to "change the evidence provided by the witness but to modify the manner in which the evidence is conveyed to the audience" (Myers & Arena, 2001, p. 389). Trial consultants help witnesses to improve their communication skills and provide training on factors that influence the effectiveness and persuasiveness of presentations, such as eye contact, hesitation, stuttering, hand placement, and fidgeting, as well as the importance of consistent and clear responses. If the attorney asks practice questions, the trial consultant may review the effectiveness of the witness's responses. Trial consultants might employ mock jurors to respond to the practice testimony and provide assistance in improving the witness's presentation style (Nietzel & Dillehay, 1986). Part of their job entails helping the witness to understand his or her feelings about the issues of the case, courtroom environment, direct examination, and cross-examination (Nietzel & Dillehay, 1986). The trial consultant also may assist the attorney in determining what strategy to use in questioning the witness (e.g., Should the witness provide long, narrative responses, or short ones?).

Trial strategy. Trial consultants assist attorneys in devising strategies for trial presentation. Using focus groups, trial consultants assess people's reactions to the evidence and to the attorney's presentation style. They then provide advice on how to present the evidence in the most favorable light, given people's natural tendencies and biases. Psychological research suggests that the information provided in an attorney's opening statement is very important in influencing juror's perceptions of the case (Nietzel & Dillehay, 1986); therefore, trial consultants provide attorneys with advice on how to present opening statements, as well as closing statements. In short, trial consultants employ what we've learned from psychological research about attitude formation and change to help attorneys present a strong case.

Advantages and Disadvantages of a Career in Trial Consulting

Trial consulting enables psychologists who are interested in legal issues to apply psychological knowledge within legal contexts. One of the main advantages of a career in trial consulting is that it is intellectually stimulating and requires knowledge and the ability to apply information from many areas of psychology: social psychology (e.g., persuasion, attitude formation and change), experimental psychology (e.g., survey methodology), statistics, counseling (e.g., listening skills, communication skills training), and many others.

A career in trial consulting can require long hours and be stressful. Trial dates can be unpredictable and frequently research data and conclusions are needed on very short notice. The tight deadlines can be particularly grueling. In addition, some psychologists who have entered trial consulting explain that it entails a steep learning curve because most of the learning is through trial and error and experience rather than simply book-knowledge (DeAngelis, 2001). For example, trial consultant Joy Stapp (1996) explains that, "Although I knew how to do research, I knew only a little about lawyers, almost nothing about the law, and zero about marketing." Psychologists may be surprised at how much there is to learn, but may also find such learning fascinating and rewarding.

An important advantage of a career in trial consulting is that it is lucrative. Depending on their specialty and experience, trial consultants charge from $75 to over $300 per hour (Myers & Arena, 2001). The industry is growing and shows no signs of slowing down. As Myers and Arena (2001) point out, trial consultants have a large potential client base of over 900,000 lawyers in the United States and nearly 40,000 new lawyers entering the field each year. Eighteen million new lawsuits emerge each year, so it is likely that trial consulting will continue as a growth field.

MEDIATOR

Given the backlog of cases within the U.S. court system, participants in civil suits (individuals or organizations) are encouraged to attempt to settle or resolve their dispute without the use of the court system (Wrightsman, 2001). Mediation, or alternative dispute resolution, is an alternative to traditional trial procedures that "involves a third person as an arbitrator or mediator between the disputants; the arbitrator's job is to try to reconcile disputants' claims so that they can agree on their own and avoid a trial" (Wrightsman, 2001, p. 167). Mediation has been used to settle a variety of civil cases, including sexual harassment, racial disputes, child custody, and other civil litigation.

Within a child custody case, for example, a mediator can help parents to settle on a plan for custody and visitation through a process that is less stressful for the child and best fits the child's needs. The mediator may meet with both parties together or separately and may also meet with the child(ren). In many ways, the mediator acts as a "go-between," facilitating communication between both parties by meeting separately with each. The mediator plays a similar role in other civil cases. For example, within the context of a sexual harassment case, a mediator meets with both parties to determine the events in question, and works to devise a plan to prevent future problems (e.g., shifting job responsibilities so that there is less interaction among the parties, agreements about future behaviors).

The advantages of a career as a mediator are similar to those of a trial consultant: income and growth of the field. Hourly rates for mediators can reach $380 to $450 per hour (Cooper, 2002). The increase in civil litigation means that there are plenty of opportunities for effective mediators to carve out a practice. Mediation enables a more flexible schedule than does trial consultation because mediators don't have to arrange their work around court dates. Finally, a potential disadvantage to a career in mediation is that dealing with the animosity of arguing parties can be wearisome.

EXPERT WITNESS

Expert witnesses testify as part of an attorney's presentation of the evidence. Expert witnesses "possess special knowledge about a topic, knowledge that the average juror does not have"(Wrightsman, 2001, p. 32). The expert's role is "to educate the judge or jury as to the relevance of the psychological knowledge on the topic in general and the specific psychological findings relevant to the questions being asked in the particular case"(Walker, 1990, p. 351).

Psychologists may be called to testify on a variety of issues. In Chapter 2 we discussed the forensic evaluation activities of psychologists; some forensic psychologists are asked to supplement their reports of their findings and conclusions with courtroom testimony. Other psychologists who engage in applied research (applying psychological knowledge to solve real world problems) are asked to provide testimony related to their areas of research (e.g., battered woman syndrome, pretrial publicity impact on juries, effects of various custody arrangements on children after divorce, factors that might influence a false confession). The expert witness acts as educator in that he or she provides testimony that explains complicated psychological issues to help the jurors to understand the issues and uncover the truth.

Some of the topics that psychologists are called to testify about include: eyewitness identification (e.g., How accurate is eyewitness identification and what are the factors that influence the accuracy of eyewitness identification?), negligence and product liability (e.g., Does the environment or our perceptual abilities influence how we use products or what precautions we take in using products?), trademark litigation (e.g., Is a product's name or packaging so similar to a competitor's that it may be confusing for consumers? Are advertising claims misleading?), social issues in litigation (e.g., Can elements of one's situation, such as exposure to violence, pornography, or the experience of abuse, influence the behavior of a defendant?) and more (Neitzel & Dillehay, 1986). The expert's job is to present a balanced and neutral view of the relevant literature (Bruck, 1998) and draw conclusions based on scientifically validated methodologies and theoretical positions (Rotgers & Barrett, 1996). Given psychology's emphasis on understanding human behavior, the topics on which psychologists may provide expert testimony are endless.

If you're considering a career as an expert witness, recognize that most psychologists who provide expert testimony do so as one of many roles. For example, researchers and college professors provide expert testimony regarding areas of their research. Unless you become a forensic evaluator (see Chapter 2), it's unlikely that you will devote your career to providing expert testimony. Instead, your role as an expert witness will be one of the many roles that you'll fulfill as a psychologist (e.g., educator, researcher, clinician). With that said, expert testimony provides many advantages for qualified psychologists. One of the most salient being income. Expert witnesses may earn as much as $500 per hour, depending on specialty area and experience (Wrightsman et al., 2002).

Taking the witness stand is challenging, to say the least. As Chappelle and Rosengren (2001) point out:

> A skilled attorney may overtly challenge the expert witness's training, education, or experience, and suggest that his or her opinion is no better than casual 'guesswork.' An attorney may reject the validity of the testimony in an atmosphere of ridicule, sarcasm, and contempt. The attorney may attempt to 'rattle' the expert witness by using a strong tone of voice, directive questions, gestures, intimidating eye contact, and dramatic interpersonal posturing. (p. 52)

Providing testimony can cause anxiety and self doubt (Neitzel & Dillehay, 1986) because the cross-examination will likely challenge your experience, credentials, person, and the validity of your professional work. Lloyd-Bostock (1988) explains that, "the treatment psychologists… are sometimes exposed to in the witness box can come as a shock to the unprepared" (p. 432). Providing testimony can be both intimidating and exciting, and requires professionalism and emotional control. Many psychologists thrive within an adversarial courtroom environment, while others dread it.

A potential disadvantage to becoming an expert witness is a loss of privacy in one's professional and personal life. Cross-examining attorneys may attempt to discredit you in the eyes of the jury by reading excerpts of your articles aloud, citing information from your interviews or television appearances, and any other information that they can find to demonstrate inconsistency in your work, opinions, and conclusions. Essentially this means that if you decide to provide expert testimony, you must carefully examine your career for any information (professional or personal) that might be used to discredit you (Reid, 1999).

Nevertheless, serving as an expert witness is intellectually stimulating and, for some, invigorating. It also poses interesting ethical challenges. Although the psychologist has been hired and paid by an attorney, he or she must remain objective and accurate in his or her responses. It's hard not to be sympathetic toward one side or another, so maintaining objectivity can be a challenge. However, maintaining objectivity is an essential part of an expert witness's job, especially since juries are likely to view psychologists as advocates, not objective, unbiased scientists.

A final challenge is coping with the fact that the nature of law and psychology often collide. The law expects firm either/or decisions, while psychology discusses probabilities and likelihoods. In other words, "The law requires the psychologist to reach a firm conclusion on the witness stand, regardless of ambiguity in the evidence" (Wrightsman et al., 2002, p. 44). As a student of psychology, you've come to understand that behavior is influenced by multiple factors and that there is rarely one cause to a particular behavior or event. Psychologists who take the witness stand must traverse the ambiguity to arrive at conclusions, then explain how they arrived at the conclusions as well as the limiting factors. This is a difficult task indeed.

SUGGESTED READINGS

Bennett, C. E., & Hirschhorn, R. (1993). *Bennett's guide to jury selection & trial dynamics in civil & criminal litigation.* Eagan, MN: West.

Brodsky, S. L. (1991). *Testifying in court: Guidelines and maxims for the expert witness.* Washington, DC: American Psychological Association.

Brodsky, S. L. (1999). *The expert expert witness: More maxims and guidelines for testifying in court.* Washington, DC: American Psychological Association.

Ceci, S. J., & Hembrooke, H. (1998). *Expert witnesses in child abuse cases: What can and should be said in court.* Washington, DC: American Psychological Association.

Hess, A. K. (1999). Serving as an expert witness. In A. K. Hess & I. B. Weiner (Eds.), *The handbook of forensic psychology* (pp. 521–555). New York: Wiley.

Myers, B., & Arena, M. P. (2001). Trial consultation: A new direction in applied psychology. *Professional Psychology: Research and Practice, 32,* 386–391.

Nietzel, M. T., & Dillehay, R. C. (1986). *Psychological consultation in the courtroom.* New York: Pergamon.

Poynter, D. (1997). *Expert witness handbook: Tips and techniques for the litigation consultant.* Santa Barbara: Para.

Stapp, J. (1996). An interesting career in psychology: Trial consultant. *Psychological Science Agenda.* Retrieved on August 15, 2002, at http://www.apa.org/science/ic-stapp.html

WEB RESOURCES

American Society of Trial Consultants
http://www.astcweb.org/

Law and Psychiatry Columns
http://www.reidpsychiatry.com/columns.html

Mediation.com
http://www.mediate.com

What do you know? Psychologist Reviews Divorce Mediation
http://www.divorcemed.com/Articles/WhatDoYouKnow.htm

PROFILE 4.1 : ERIC G. MART, PH.D.

Dr. Eric G. Mart is a licensed psychologist in private practice in Manchester, New Hampshire. He is an internationally known expert on Munchausen's Syndrome by Proxy and has testified on the subject in court cases throughout the United States and Canada. He is certified as a school psychologist by the New Hampshire State Board of Education and is certified by the American Psychological Association in the Treatment of Alcohol and Other Substance Abuse Disorders.

Dr. Mart specializes in forensic psychology and also sees children, adolescents, adults, and couples for psychotherapy and testing. In his forensic work, investigative techniques based on empirical research and established protocols are emphasized. This methodology is designed to provide information that is maximally useful to the courts and that enables the parties involved to understand how conclusions were reached and what data were used.

Dr. Mart provided responses to several questions I posed concerning his work in forensic psychology, views of the benefits and challenges of the field, and advice for undergraduate students.

What originally got you interested in the field of forensic psychology?

I actually didn't know there was such a specialty except in the vaguest terms until 1985, when I met Wilfrid Derby, Ph.D., ABPP (Forensic and Clinical). He suggested that I get involved in the area, trained me, and supplied me with referrals until I had a practice and reputation in my own right. He also encouraged me to obtain the ABPP in forensic psych and supervised me (free of charge) until I received it in April 2001. Dr. Derby is and continues to be as the ancient Greeks used to say, the father of my art and mentor.

Describe what activities you are involved in as a forensic psychologist.

My private practice includes many areas of forensic psychology. For example, I conduct criminal and civil competency tests (e.g., competency to stand trial or to waive Miranda rights), offender evaluations, and risk assessments (i.e., estimates of the risk a particular offender poses). I also consult on personal injury cases (e.g., determining emotional or psychological trauma), child custody cases, and probate cases (i.e., determining an individual's competence to establish or modify a will).

I go to court at least 2–3 times per month and am often deposed by attorneys. My evaluations are mostly conducted in my office, but I also go to prisons, jails, and hospitals. I have testified in courts throughout the United States and several places in Canada, and I have consulted on cases in South Africa, New Zealand and Australia. When my articles on MSBP [Munchausen's Syndrome by Proxy] came out, I appeared on 20/20, Court TV, and BBC radio. I think it might have been my 15 minutes of fame.

What is being in court like?

It is intense and sometimes anxiety provoking, but I enjoy it. I like the adversarial nature of testifying in court and actually look forward to a good cross-examination. It reminds me of sports in my younger days, when a wrestling meet or fencing match heightened my awareness and brought out my best performance.

Describe the advantages and disadvantages to a career in forensic psychology.

A career in forensic psychology is intellectually stimulating. I have the opportunity to meet and interact with a broad range of people and my work involves analytical thinking and problem solving. Providing testimony within the courtroom offers additional challenges and rewards because the court is an adversarial environment. It's essential to remain current in your field and to project your expertise with professionalism and confidence. The courtroom requires a certain level of composure; in a sense it's like a performance, which can be an advantage or disadvantage, depending on your perspective and personality. Other advantages of forensic psychology are that it is lucrative and a growth field, as many forensic subspecialties are emerging.

What advice would you give to a student considering a career in forensic psychology?

First and foremost is to develop a firm foundation in scientific psychology. All too often undergraduates enroll in the "fun courses," like abnormal psychology and neglect the experimentally oriented areas of psychology as well as the overall history of psychology. It is essential that you learn about empirical research. You don't need to be the best researcher, but you need to comprehend research well enough to be able to read journal articles and understand what you're reading.

Develop your analytic skills because forensic psychology is a hard-nosed specialty—you must be able to defend the empirical bases of your conclusions in court. During graduate school, learn about the law. A law degree isn't necessary, but you should have a basic understanding of the legal terms that you'll encounter in your work. If you're considering a high-power forensic career (e.g., as a law professor), a combination J.D./Ph.D. program will offer you a comprehensive background in both psychology and law.

PSYCHOLOGISTS AS SOCIAL ACTIVISTS

5

CHAPTER GUIDE

Many psychologists are interested in influencing public policy decisions, or decisions about issues that affect the quality of human life, such as health care, education, welfare, crime and violence prevention, and other social issues (Levant et al., 2001). Psychology holds a tremendous potential for informing decisions made in the legal system and bringing about legal reform when necessary (Wrightsman, 2001). As Fowler (1996) eloquently explains, psychologists offer many contributions to the development of public policy:

> At the initial stage, when a social problem is identified and being defined, psychologists can question assumptions about human behavior, provide scientific data, and present alternative formulations. In policy formation, when a plan is being developed to solve the problem, psychologists can synthesize the available literature on interventions, design pilot studies, and evaluate possible alternative policies. At the stage when legislators are working for adoption of a measure, psychologists can provide help in organization, networking, and other types of communication and interpersonal influence. At the implementation stage, particularly when psychologists are part of the programs to be implemented, psychologists bring all their intervention and treatment skills to bear. Finally, at the stage when the effectiveness and impact of a policy is being evaluated, psychologists' research skills are particularly relevant. (p. ix).

RESEARCH PSYCHOLOGISTS AND PUBLIC POLICY

Psychologists conduct research that sheds light on important social problems (e.g., the impact of welfare reform on low-income families). Psychologists who conduct policy-related research may work within traditional academic settings (i.e., colleges and universities), government positions (e.g., National Institutes of Mental Health, National Institute on Drug Abuse), and at think tanks or policy-oriented organizations that resemble academia (Kuther & Morgan, 2004).

Psychologists with policy interests might lobby and inform legislators about their research findings as well as other relevant findings from the psychology literature. Other research psychologists (regardless of work setting, academic or otherwise) might provide expert testimony during Congressional hearings to educate legislators about psychological issues that bear on public policy (Wrightsman, 2001). Research psychologists may be asked to participate in committees to draft *amicus curiae* briefs on behalf of the American Psychological Association (a professional organization for psychologists). An *amicus curiae* brief is "a stylized instrument for combining facts, law, and logic as needed to present judges with the most compelling argument for adopting whatever position the filer advocates" (Tremper, 1987, p. 496). In other words, it's a formal way of educating legislators about psychological findings pertinent to a particular case.

Research psychologists within academia may engage in any of these activities as an extension of their policy-related research. As we discussed in Chapter 1, academic careers offer a flexible schedule, autonomy, and prestige. Disadvantages of a research career in academia include competition (i.e., academic positions are scarce), long hours, and the pressure to publish. Many psychologists engage in public policy research careers outside of academia. Research psychologists employed at nonprofit agencies and think tanks conduct research to assess and improve the agency's effectiveness (e.g., in creating policy-related programs, such as programs to promote work-related skills for low-income clients), examine social problems and potential solutions, and lobby legislative bodies. Nonprofit agencies and think tanks often are contracted by the government to conduct policy analyses, literature reviews, and research to improve decision making by political leaders and consumers. If you choose a career in public policy at a nonprofit or think tank, much of your time will be spent writing grants, conducting research, analyzing the impact of various policies, and writing, presenting, and publishing your work in various formats to ensure that your findings are accessible to the public and to policy makers. See Box 5.1 for examples of think tanks and public policy organizations.

**BOX
5.1**   **POLICY-ORIENTED ORGANIZATIONS AND THINK TANKS**

Perhaps the best way to gain perspective on research careers in think tanks is to explore three prominent policy oriented organizations. Remember that these are just a small sampling of the policy centers that abound.

- RAND (the acronym is a contraction of the term "research and development") is the oldest think tank, created in 1946 (http://www.rand.org/about/). The mission of RAND, like other think tanks, is to apply research and analysis to improve policy and decision making. RAND, a very large organization, conducts policy research in a variety of areas. Projects have included creating a nationwide drug prevention program for school children, evaluating the quality of health care for older adults, and assessing the impact of Indonesia's economic crisis on its citizens.

- The Families and Work Institute is a research center that provides data about the interaction of work and family to inform decision making. Researchers at the Families and Work Institute conduct research on "work-life issues and concerns confronting workers and employers in order to inform decision makers in government, business, communities, and families" (Families and Work Institute, n.d.). Sample projects include longitudinal studies with nationally representative samples of U.S. workers to learn about the changing nature of work, longitudinal studies of employers to understand how U.S. employers are responding to employee work-life needs, and interviews with children to understand how they make sense of their world and the implications for schools, programs, and policies.

BOX 5.1   *(CONTINUED)*

- Manpower Demonstration Research Corporation (MDRC) is "dedicated to learning what works to improve the well-being of low-income people" (http://www.mdrc.org/) and actively communicating findings to enhance the effectiveness of public policies and programs. Researchers at MDRC conduct evaluations of welfare reforms and other supports for the working poor as well as research on how programs affect children's development and their families' well-being. Other projects examine the effectiveness of school reform policies designed to improve academic achievement and access to college, and community approaches to increasing employment in low-income neighborhoods.

(From Kuther & Morgan, 2004)

The primary benefit of conducting policy-related research is that your work may lead to social change. Policy research is interdisciplinary in nature, which means that research psychologists in think tanks work with a diverse range of specialists in other fields. Researchers in think tanks and policy-oriented organizations earn salaries similar to those in academia (see Chapter 1). In 1999, for example, doctoral degree holders with two to four years of experience earned a median salary of $55,000 in nonprofit research settings (Williams, Wicherski, & Kohout, 2000).

CONGRESSIONAL FELLOW OR STAFF MEMBER

Psychologists are valued on Capitol Hill. Some psychologists get involved in politics by assisting members of Congress as congressional fellows or as staff members. The American Psychological Association Congressional Fellow program provides psychologists with policy experience and prepares them for careers in politics. Goals of the APA Congressional Fellowship program are: "(a) to enable scientists to share their knowledge with legislators so that these lawmakers might be better able to make policies based on professional expertise, and (b) to allow scientists to share with colleagues in their field an 'insider's' understanding of the policy-making process and their potential role in it" (Vincent, 1990, p. 61).

Fellows serve a one- or two-year assignment to a staff position in Congress. They perform as regular staff members and are involved in legislative, investigative, and oversight activities. They may develop briefs, conduct psycholegal research, and become involved in planning strategies and drafting laws (American Psychological Association, 2002). Congressional fellows participate in face-to-face briefings with members of Congress, assist in providing information for legislation debated on the floor of the House or Senate, and represent the congressperson at meetings with lobbyists and constituents (Fowler, 1996). About half of fellows later take policy-related positions with federal agencies, Congress, or policy research organizations (Fowler, 1996).

Advantages of a congressional fellowship or staff member position include firsthand participation in policy formation, promoting social change, and making a difference. Psychologists who choose this career path must become generalists in the sense that they will deal with volumes of information on a wide array of subjects. A policy career is fast paced and toilsome, but rewarding. Entry-level psychologist fellows in the American Psychological Association Fellowship program earn approximately $48,500 with a range increasing to $63,100, depending on experience. For information about other congressional fellowship programs, see Box 5.2.

BOX 5.2   PUBLIC POLICY FELLOWSHIP PROGRAMS

APA Congressional Fellowship Program
http://www.apa.org/ppo/funding/congfell.html

Catherine Acuff Congressional Fellowship
http://www.apa.org/ppo/funding/cathfell.html

Society for Research in Child Development: Congressional and Executive Branch Fellowships
http://www.srcd.org/policyfellowships.html

American Association for the Advancement of Science: Policy Fellowships
http://fellowships.aaas.org/

William A. Bailey AIDS Policy Congressional Fellowship
http://www.apa.org/ppo/funding/baileyfell.html

White House Fellows Program
http://www.whitehouse.gov/fellows/

POLITICAL CONSULTANT

Some psychologists with political and legal interests become political consultants. Political consultants come from all walks of life and disciplines (e.g., political science, history), but psychologists offer unique skills that are valued by politicians. Politics deals with people, and who better understands people than psychologists? Psychologists who work as political consultants are hired by politicians to conduct surveys to gather information about public opinions, provide advice about how to address volatile issues that affect voters, and to guide political campaigns. In other words, political consultants are very much like trial consultants (Chapter 4), but instead of preparing witnesses and lawyers for the courtroom, they prepare politicians for public appearances and conduct research (e.g., polls, public opinion surveys) to assist with campaigns and garner public support. Political consultants might draft speeches or articles for the op-ed pages of newspapers, assist politicians in handling bad press, and help politicians to hone their messages and communicate effectively with voters (American Association of Political Consultants, n.d.).

There is a large client base for political consultants because "every two years, there are more than 450,000 political races and 1.5 million candidates across the U.S." (Pamintuan, 2000). Careers as political consultants are fast paced and stressful. Polling and opinion surveys must be conducted quickly and conclusions must be drawn immediately to assist politicians in brisk political races. Although salary information is hard to come by for political consultants, it's a safe bet to estimate high salaries (similar to those of trial consultants), given the specialized nature of the work. Finally, a career as a political consultant is intellectually stimulating because it requires being up-to-date on current events, politics, and public policy.

SUGGESTED READINGS

Appelgate, D. (1993). Science and public policy: Translating between two worlds. In C. Robbins-Roth (Ed.), *Alternative careers in science.* New York: Academic Press.

Celeste, B. L. (2000). We must be the change we want to see in the world: Psychologists in the statehouse. *Professional Psychology: Research & Practice, 31*(5), 469–472.

Copper, C. (1997) An interesting career in psychology: Social science analyst in the public sector. *Psychological Science Agenda.* Retrieved on August 16, 2002, at: http://www.apa.org/science/ic-copper.html

Flattau, P. E. (1998). An interesting career in psychology: Policy scientist as an independent consultant. *Psychological Science Agenda.* Retrieved on August 16, 2002, at: http://www.apa.org/science/ic-flattau.html

Griffin, J. A. (2001). An interesting career in psychology: A psychologist in the White House. *Psychological Science Agenda.* Retrieved on August 16, 2002, at http://www.apa.org/science/ic-griffin.html

Lee, J. A., DeLeon, P. H., Wedding, D., & Nordal, K. (1994). Psychologists' role in influencing Congress: The process and the players. *Professional Psychology: Research & Practice, 25*(1), 9–15.

Monroe, K. R. (2002). *Political psychology.* Mahwah, NJ: Erlbaum.

Walley, P. B. (1995). Lucky dogs. Professional *Psychology: Research & Practice, 26*(5), 459–461.

Weiner, H. R. (2001). An interesting career in psychology: Expert witness in employment discrimination cases. *Psychological Science Agenda.* Retrieved on August 16, 2002, at http://www.apa.org/science/ic-weiner.html

WEB RESOURCES

Advancing the Science: A Psychologist's Guide to Advocacy
http://www.apa.org/science/advancescience.html

A Psychologist's Guide to Participation in Federal Policymaking
http://www.apa.org/ppo/grassroots/padguide.html

Speak up for yourself!
http://www.apa.org/monitor/jan01/speakup.html

Psychology's state-level legislators
http://www.apa.org/monitor/mar01/statelevel.html

The National Research Council
http://www.nas.edu/nrc/

International Society of Political Psychology
http://ispp.org/

Center for the Study of Political Psychology
http://www.polisci.umn.edu/polipsyc/about/projects.html

PROFILE 5.1 : SCYATTA A. WALLACE, PH.D.

Dr. Wallace received her BA in Psychology from Yale University and her doctorate in Developmental Psychology from Fordham University. She is currently an Oak Ridge Institute for Science and Education (ORISE) research fellow at the Centers for Disease Control and Prevention in the Division of HIV/AIDS Prevention. At CDC, she is assisting with the development of an early intervention for African American parents of young adolescents to promote sexual risk reduction.

Her research interests include delineating cultural and contextual factors that may be useful for youth-focused prevention efforts in communities of color. She has extensive research experience working with African American populations. In addition, she has worked with several organizations, serving as a consultant program evaluator with Columbia University School of Public Health (ETAC), the African American Studies Department at Fordham University, and the Social Science Research Council Mellon Minority program. Dr. Wallace has authored and coauthored several peer reviewed journal articles, has been featured in two issues of the *APA Monitor,* and has been recognized with numerous fellowships and scholarship awards. Dr. Wallace answered several questions regarding her experience and provided advice for students.

How did you become interested in social policy relevant research?

All my life I've been exposed to politics and leadership in government. My family, which immigrated to the United States from Liberia, West Africa, had a long history of public service in government. By observing my family members, including my father, I was able to see how government can work for the greater good of the people it serves. During my childhood and adolescence I became greatly involved in activism and community service. However, I didn't seek out public policy endeavors until I began graduate school in Applied Developmental Psychology. It was there that I was exposed to social policy due to the program's strong focus on how developmental research could be made relevant to policy efforts. I realized that this area was of interest to me and sought to find some hands-on experience in the field.

Describe your fellowship. How did you learn about it and what did you do?

I was a member of the Society for the Psychological Study of Social Issues (SPSSI) and the American Psychological Association (APA) and enjoyed reading the publications that they issued. Social policy was on my radar screen and as I was reading the SPSSI newsletter I noticed an announce-ment about the Dalmas A. Taylor summer policy fellowship. I went through the formal application process and was given a call that I was chosen. I had no idea what a wonderful life changing experience was in store for me.

During the 8-week fellowship, sponsored by the Minority Fellowship Program at APA and SPSSI, I learned a lot about Congress, legislation, and particularly the importance of the lobbying process. I was also exposed to many psychologists who chose multiple career paths that are related to public interest. I was housed in the APA Public Policy office working with Adrienne Stith, Ph.D., SPSSI Public Policy Fellow 1999–2000, Lori Valencia Green, Senior Legislative/Federal Affairs Officer, and Ellen Garrison, Ph.D., Director, Public Interest Policy. Part of my learning experience involved reading important policy publications and watching Senate and House de-bates on CSPAN. I also attended many congressional briefings sponsored by various organizations to educate the public, press, and congressional staff about issues concerning current legislative initiatives. For example, I attended a briefing sponsored by the Consortium of Social Science Asso-ciations (COSSA) and the National Consortium on Violence Research (NCOVR). They invited three distinguished researchers/experts to speak to Congress about controlling violence in America. In addition, I attended con-gressional hearings, which provide multiple witnesses who can assist Con-gress in making informed decisions regarding legislation.

The majority of my work focused on an amendment to the Health Care Fairness Act of 1999. This legislation (H.R. 3250 and S. 1880) was devel-oped to address health disparities in communities of color and medically underserved populations. Specifically the bills were targeted to increase the amount of research regarding ethnic minority health and health dispar-ities, including developing cultural competency training for health profes-sionals. My role as a fellow was to assist in getting these bills passed into legislation in a manner that spoke to the needs of the underserved commu-nities and those that serve them. My first assignment was to review the health disparity legislation (H.R. 3250 and S. 1880). I compared both the House and Senate versions and made comments and remarks regarding the content. I made weekly visits to congressional offices to inform and ed-ucate congressional staff on the importance of including behavioral sci-ence in the content of the bill. I began creating facts sheets, which included examples of current behavioral health research, to be used during those congressional visits. In addition, I assisted with preparations for a briefing the APA sponsored on racial/ethnic health disparities. By the end of my fellowship I was able to see the legislation pass in the Senate and the House. Later that year, it was signed into law and health disparities has become one of the main foci of public health efforts, as charged in "Healthy People 2010", the nation's public health agenda for the next 10 years.

What are your areas of interest or expertise?

Most of my experience has been in adolescent risk research. Specifically I have been involved in many research projects examining factors associated with youth involvement in violence, substance use, and HIV/AIDS risk. I am particularly interested in identifying unique cultural protective factors that can be implemented in prevention efforts targeting Black American youth. My policy interest is to serve as an advocate for public health efforts serving disadvantaged populations by informing key policy makers and assisting community-based efforts.

How has the fellowship influenced your later work?

The Dalmas A. Taylor summer policy experience allowed me to see from start to finish how behavioral research is relevant to social policy. It led me to realize I could balance my interest in prevention research and social policy as a career. In addition, the fellowship opened my eyes to the transferability and utility of my training in developmental psychology. The fellowship changed my career focus from an academic one to a public health framework. Currently, I am beginning a research fellowship at the Centers for Disease Control and Prevention in the Division of HIV/AIDS Prevention. It is the perfect interface between policy and research. CDC conducts research and develops programs that promote public health for the nation. The research and programs are based on strategic plans developed by the Administration. Therefore, the work we do is policy driven and in turn our research is used to inform future policy initiatives. I've committed myself to staying active in social policy and serving as an additional voice for the marginalized communities that I work with.

What are the advantages and disadvantages of policy work?

The advantage of conducting social policy relevant research is that it can impact large populations of people. Many social policy agendas are set to influence laws for the whole nation. For this reason it can be extremely gratifying work, with the satisfaction of seeing the results of your work improving the lives of many people. The disadvantage is that this line of work often leads to compromise. Regardless of the intentions of the policy initiatives, we live in a democratic society where all sides have to agree in order for legislation to move forward. This means that often the original intent of the work will greatly change by the time it reaches the president to be signed. In a lot of cases, useful and important legislation never makes it to the congressional floor or gets forgotten in more hotly contested debates. This is especially the case in my line of research, where sensitive topics are the focus (e.g., teen sex, adolescent drug use, racial/cultural issues). The controversial nature of the topics can override the intent of the research, the urgent need in the target communities, and the scientific bases of the project. Therefore, doing social policy relevant research takes a lot of patience, good communication skills, and thick skin. I try to never take things personally and stay grounded in my goal to promote health and decrease health disparities in communities of color.

What advice would you give to students?

Read, read, read! This includes congressional periodicals, newspapers, and politically relevant websites. Learn about current events and how they impact the decisions that are made in government. Talk with your local representatives and find out what they are doing and what legislation they are currently working on that may be relevant to your interests. Watch C-SPAN. It is very educative, you will learn a lot about how laws are made in congress. There are some great policy focused think tanks, such as the Joint Center for Poverty Research. These institutions have publications that would be a great resource for learning about policy relevant research. Think out of the box because many academic institutions do not favor nonacademic career tracks. Try to find a mentor in social policy and with whom you can develop a plan that will steer you closer to your goal.

Is Psychology and Law for You?

Chapter Guide

Throughout this book we've explored various career paths in forensic and legal psychology: forensic assessment, trial consulting, expert witnessing, correctional and police psychology, public policy, politics, and careers in academia. As you've seen, there are many exciting career opportunities in the field of psychology and law. In this chapter, we extend our discussion to training opportunities in psychology and law: how do you get to where you'd like to be, career-wise? We'll discuss master's degrees and doctoral degrees, the many paths to a career in psychology and law, and what you can do now, as an undergraduate, to prepare for your career in psychology and law.

GRADUATE TRAINING IN PSYCHOLOGY AND THE LAW

Master's Degrees

If you're considering graduate study in psychology and law, do some research and learn about the various degree options available to you. Your advisor is a good source of information, but also do your own research because advisors often know little about master's degrees in psychology (Actkinson, 2000), despite its popularity. About 13,000 students receive master's degrees in psychology each year (Hays-Thomas, 2000). In fact, a far greater number of students pursue master's degrees than doctoral degrees (Kuther, 2003).

The master's degree typically is awarded after 2 years of study beyond the bachelor's degree. There are many different types of master's degrees, but the most common are the M.A. (master of arts) and M.S. (master of science). Although there is usually no substantive difference between an M.A. and an M.S., some universities or departments award only one or the other. In the psychology departments that award both, an M.A. may require a thesis and an M.S. may substitute additional statistics and research courses and a comprehensive exam for the thesis—but this is not always the case (Lloyd, 1997).

So what can you do with a master's degree? Students who are interested in psychology and law seek master's degrees to become more competitive for jobs in government, social policy, and politics, or to practice clinical or counseling psychology under supervision within correctional, police, and other forensic settings. Depending on the particular state, graduates of some clinical and counseling master's programs meet the requirements for licensure as counselors or marriage and family therapists (Levant, Moldawsky, & Stigall, 2000). Exactly what you choose to do with your master's degree depends on your graduate experiences and the field in which you've earned your degree. If you're interested in psychology and law, you've got two basic options: a master's degree in forensic psychology, or a master's degree in another area of psychology.

Master's degree in forensic psychology. Master's programs in forensic psychology prepare students to analyze, interpret, organize, apply, and disseminate knowledge in the field of forensic psychology. Typically, students are trained to become mental health professionals, able to work in a variety of clinical settings within the criminal and civil legal system, including but not limited to: adult, juvenile, and child populations; victim assistance; police consultation; correctional institutions; domestic violence and child abuse programs; and trial consulting. Most programs focus on understanding, evaluation, and treatment of adult and juvenile offenders, as well as the victims of violence and crime.

Other master's degrees in psychology. A master's degree in psychology, regardless of area, can offer you the background needed for several types of psychology and law careers, if you plan ahead and seek appropriate academic (e.g., coursework) and field experiences (e.g., applied research or supervised practice). For example, a master's degree in clinical or counseling psychology provides training in psychological assessment and psychotherapy, enabling the graduate to provide basic mental health services within correctional and police settings (Kuther & Morgan, 2004). Additional courses in psychology and law, crisis management, and criminal justice, as well as practical experience within prisons or other correctional settings may strengthen your credentials for forensics or correctional employment.

Research-oriented master's programs, such as those in developmental, experimental, social, quantitative, or general psychology, provide training in the various methodologies and statistical analyses critical to conducting well-designed research. Solid research skills are vital to public policy careers in government and policy organizations, as well as political consulting (i.e., polling). Seek applied research experience through formal practica or volunteer to help a professor with his or her research on an applied topic. Additional courses in psychology and law, public policy, or political science will round out your background and demonstrate your interest in policy-related issues.

If you're considering a master's degree, carefully consider your career goals. In many cases, a specialized master's degree in forensic psychology may be unnecessary and may be less marketable than a master's degree in clinical or counseling psychology or another area of psychology. Why? Forensic psychology is highly specialized, which means that you may have a difficult time selling yourself to employers in fields other than corrections. A clinical or counseling degree will enable you to work in a wide range of settings. Considering that correctional settings can be stressful and lead to burnout, it's important to leave the door open for other opportunities. If you're interested in research or a policy-oriented career, seek a master's degree in developmental, social, general, quantitative or experimental psychology with additional courses in public policy, as well as applied research experience. Also consider a master's degree in public policy as an alternative to psychology.

Doctoral Degrees

A doctoral degree provides a greater range of flexibility than does a master's degree. Typically, a doctoral degree requires 5 to 7 years of graduate work. Applied areas, such as clinical and counseling psychology, also include a year or more of internship or supervised experience as a practitioner. What can you do with a doctoral degree? Any of the careers discussed within this book (with the appropriate preparation, of course). As you begin to research doctoral programs, you'll discover that there are two types of doctoral degrees in psychology: the Ph.D. and the Psy.D.

The Ph.D. The doctor of philosophy (Ph.D.) in psychology is a research degree that prepares graduates for research, university teaching, and clinical practice. Research is emphasized in Ph.D. programs; typically students engage in research with their advisors throughout the graduate program and then complete a dissertation based on their own original research. Like the master's degree, the Ph.D. is offered in a wide range of areas (e.g., developmental, experimental, quantitative, social, clinical, counseling, school, and more).

The Psy.D. The doctor of psychology (Psy.D.) is a practitioner degree that is offered only in clinical and counseling psychology. The main difference between a Ph.D. and a Psy.D. is that the Psy.D. prepares graduates to be consumers of research, rather than producers of new knowledge (Lloyd, 1997). Students in Psy.D. programs conduct lots of applied and practical work, and complete comprehensive examinations. If a dissertation is required, it is usually a theoretical or literature review paper rather than an empirical study. Seek a Psy.D. if your aim is to engage in clinical practice, rather than conduct research.

Doctoral Programs in Psychology and Law

As we've discussed with master's programs, there are several doctoral study paths that students with interests in psychology and law may take.

Traditional clinical or counseling psychology programs. Most forensic psychologists did not graduate from forensic psychology or psychology and law programs. Instead, they earned clinical or counseling degrees and then completed predoctoral or postdoctoral internships in forensic, correctional, or police psychology, and/or continuing education courses, seminars, additional course work, and supervision by a senior colleague (see Chapters 2 and 3 for more specific recommendations for training in each of these career areas).

Joint-degree programs. Students who are very interested in the law may enroll in joint programs that offer degrees in both psychology (Ph.D.) and the law (J.D., or doctor of jurisprudence). Joint-degree programs entail completing both a doctoral psychology program and law school, making the graduate a psychologist and lawyer. The goals of joint degree are to train "scholars and practitioners interested in research and policy careers who will produce theoretically and methodologically sophisticated research integrating the psychology, and policy interface" (Ogloff, Tomkins, & Bersoff, 1996, p. 217). With a joint degree, you'll get broad exposure to the law, which may open up new career possibilities. (Hafemeister, Ogloff, & Small, 1990).

An important advantage to a joint degree is the sophisticated understanding of legal issues that is imparted in such programs. A thorough understanding of legal issues is essential to conduct policy and legal research that is externally valid, credible, and able to produce change (Ogloff, 2000). Comprehensive legal education raises graduates' awareness of questions of law that relate to psychology and vice versa, expanding the scope of legal psychology inquiry to include new and innovative research topics (Ogloff et al., 1996). On the other hand, joint-degree programs require additional time, expense, and motivation to complete (Bersoff, Goodman, Delahunty & Grisso, 1997). Joint-degree programs also involve learning about aspects of the law that have limited relevance for a career in forensic psychology (e.g., real estate law) (Bersoff et al., 1997). In addition, the scope of psychology training in most joint-degree programs is too broad to prepare graduates for careers in psychology research (Ogloff et al., 1996). Despite these disadvantages, graduates of joint J.D./Ph.D. programs generally are satisfied with their training in both law and psychology (Hafemeister et al., 1990). See Box 6.1 for a list of joint J.D./Ph.D. programs.

BOX 6.1   JOINT J.D. /PH.D. PROGRAMS IN THE UNITED STATES

University of Arizona
   http://w3.arizona.edu/~psych/psylaw/description.html
Hahnemann University
   http://www.auhs.edu/shp/gradprogs/lawpsych.html
University of Nebraska-Lincoln
   http://www.unl.edu/psypage/grad/law_psychology.htm
Widener University
   http://muse.widener.edu/Graduate-Psychology/programs/
   law-psych.html

Alternatives to joint J.D./Ph.D. programs. Graduate programs offering master's degrees in legal studies (M.S.L.) or concentrations in psychology and law (i.e., a set of classes covering legal psychology) are alternatives to joint J.D./Ph.D. programs. Such programs offer a background and training in law without the financial, time, and emotional burden of completing a law degree (Ogloff et al., 1996). Typically, such programs focus on a particular content area, enabling students to obtain in-depth research experience appropriate for academic and research careers in psychology (Ogloff et al., 1996). The main disadvantage of such programs is that graduates will not be broadly knowledgeable about law (Ogloff et al., 1996); however, extensive training in law is not essential to a career as a legal psychologist (Ogloff, 2000). Instead, "It is important that psychologists who work in the legal psychology area have an in-depth understanding of the law that pertains to their own areas of work" (p. 471)

Forensic specialty programs. Within recent years, several stand-alone forensic and legal psychology Ph.D. programs have emerged. These programs are housed not within "traditional" areas of psychology, such as clinical, counseling, or social psychology, but are programs unto themselves. Carefully weigh stand-alone programs in forensic psychology and psychology and law because the field is new, training standards vary among programs, and "it is not known whether graduates of these programs are adequately prepared for the broad range of forensic practice, [or] whether they are over-specialized" (Otto, Heilbrun, & Thomas, 1990, p. 230).

When evaluating a program, be sure to ask about where recent graduates are employed. The best specialty training programs offer forensic and law coursework, forensic and psycholegal research, and practicum or predoctoral training in forensics, but not all programs are able to offer all three of these types of training experiences (Otto et al., 1990). Seek coursework in forensic assessment, law and social science, mental health policy, as well as relevant law courses (e.g., mental health law, criminal law, civil law). A few courses in law are important because they will enable you to become familiar with the law's approach to problem solving. Seek internship and practica placements in forensic settings, such as prisons, jails, court clinics, and community mental health centers that offer forensic services (Otto et al., 1990).

**BOX
6.2**   **DOCTORAL SPECIALTY PROGRAMS IN FORENSIC PSYCHOLOGY AND
PSYCHOLOGY AND LAW**

Sam Houston State University
 http://www.shsu.edu/cjcenter/forensic/forensic.htm
University of Alabama
 http://psychology.ua.edu/law.html
University of Illinois at Chicago
 http://www.uic.edu/depts/psch/psychlaw/
University of Kansas
 http://www.ukans.edu/~psycgrad/index.html

An advantage of specialty training is exposure to both psychology and law. Graduates of specialty programs gain the skills to deliver assessment and therapeutic services in forensic settings, and can conduct methodologically sound and externally valid forensic research, given their training in psychology and exposure to legal issues (Otto et al., 1990). Similar to alternative legal education and psychology programs, the main disadvantage is that graduates of specialty programs will not be broadly knowledgeable about law (Ogloff et al., 1996). See Box 6.2 for a list of specialty programs in forensic psychology and psychology and law (i.e., specializations and concentrations within traditional psychology programs, such as clinical, counseling, or social psychology) and Box 6.3 for stand-alone degree programs in forensic and legal psychology.

**BOX
6.3**   **STAND-ALONE DEGREE PROGRAMS IN FORENSIC
AND LEGAL PSYCHOLOGY**

Alliant University (Ph.D. and Psy.D. in Forensic Psychology)
 http://www.alliant.edu/ssps/forensic/
Florida International Univeristy (Ph.D. in Legal Psychology)
 http://www.fiu.edu/~koveram/legalpsy.html
Castle State College (M.A. in Forensic Psychology)
 http://www.csc.vsc.edu/psych/ForensicMasters.html
Marymount Univeristy, Arlington, VA (M.A. in Forensic Psychology)
 http://www.marymount.edu/academic/sehs/ps/forensic.html
John Jay College (M.A. in Forensic Psychology)
 http://web.jjay.cuny.edu/%7Epsy/mafaq.html

BOX 6.3   (*CONTINUED*)

University of Texas at El Paso (Ph.D. in Psychology and Law)
http://www.utep.edu/psych/psyclaw.html

Sage College (M.A. in Forensic Psychology)
http://www.sage.edu/divisions/psych/forensicpsych.html

Univeristy of Denver (M.A. in Forensic Psychology)
http://www.du.edu/gspp/ma_programdescription.html

Traditional psychology doctoral program. As Ogloff (2000) points out, "Because of the potential breadth of topics included under the legal psychology umbrella, many people do legal psychology research or practice without realizing it." (p. 467). In other words, many psychologists conduct research that has legal and policy implications (e.g., memory as applied to eyewitness testimony, impact of stress on behavior among police and correctional officers, effects of poverty and low socioeconomic status on child development), without a background in psychology and law or forensic psychology. If your goal is an academic career, a traditional graduate program in psychology (e.g., developmental, social, cognitive, experimental, clinical, or counseling psychology) is your best choice. As an academic, you may examine issues relevant to social policy and the law, provide courtroom expert testimony about your areas of expertise (see Chapter 4), and engage in other forensic and policy-related consulting work (see Chapters 4 and 5).

ADVANCING YOUR CAREER: WHAT YOU CAN DO NOW

So, you think that a career in legal or forensic psychology is for you. What can you do now, as an undergraduate, to prepare for such a career?

- **Take relevant undergraduate courses.** Enroll in courses in criminology, criminal law, statistics, research methods, social psychology, abnormal psychology, industrial/organizational psychology, public policy, and psychology of motivation.
- **Seek research experience.** Assist professors with their research or develop an independent research project. Psycholegal research or applied research is especially useful, but any research experience will help you to grow as a scholar. Research experience demonstrates your ability to work independently, as well as strengthens your analytical and critical thinking

skills. It also provides graduate admissions committees with evidence of your motivation, initiative and willingness to go beyond basic requirements.

- **Enhance your communication skills.** Take courses in English, writing, and communications. Learn how to make effective oral and written presentations.
- **Get internship experience.** Seek an undergraduate internship. Many correctional facilities accept college interns, and there are many internship opportunities within policy and political organizations. An internship or practicum will provide you with hands-on experience as well as the chance to sample a potential career and discover what psychology and law careers are really about.

Remember that there are also a variety of psychology-related positions that you can obtain with your undergraduate degree. If you're not sure whether graduate school or forensic psychology is for you, consider entry-level jobs for graduates with an undergraduate degree in psychology (See Box 6.4). Graduate education isn't always necessary for a psychology-related career in criminal justice. Of course, graduate education opens the doors to many different positions as well as to career advancement, but whether to pursue graduate education is your choice, depending on where it fits with your career goals, interests, and life. Take your time with this decision, explore your interests and options, and be true to yourself to find a career that you'll find rewarding and fulfilling.

BOX 6.4

PSYCHOLOGY AND LAW–RELATED POSITIONS FOR GRADUATES WITH A BACHELOR'S DEGREE IN PSYCHOLOGY

Activities coordinator

Affirmative action officer

Behavioral specialist

Caseworker

Child protection worker

Claims specialist

Community outreach worker

Community relations officer

Corrections officer

Crisis intervention counselor

Human resources coordinator/manager/specialist

BOX 6.4   (*CONTINUED*)

Juvenile detention worker

Mental health assistant

Police officer

Special features writer/reporter

Probation officer

Rehabilitation counselor

Substance abuse counselor

Youth counselor

(Note that some positions require additional training)

From Kuther, 2003.

SUGGESTED READINGS

Huss, M. T. (2001). Psychology and law, now and in the next century: The promise of an emerging area of psychology. In J. S. Halonen & S. F. Davis (Eds.), *The Many Faces of Psychological Research in the 21st Century.* Society for the Teaching of Psychology. Retrieved on June 18, 2003, at http://teachpsych.lemoyne.edu/teachpsych/faces/text/Ch11.htm

Huss, M. T. (2001). What is forensic psychology? It's not *Silence of the Lambs! Eye on Psi Chi,* 5(3), 25–27. (available at http://www.psichi.org/content/publications/eye/volume/vol_5/5_3/huss.asp)

Kuther, T. L. (2003). *The psychology major's handbook.* Pacific Grove, CA: Wadsworth

Kuther, T. L., & Morgan, R. (2004). *Extending the boundaries of psychology: Career opportunities in a changing world.* Pacific Grove, CA: Wadsworth.

Tomkins, A. J., & Ogloff, J. R. (1990). Training and career options in psychology and law. *Behavioral Sciences & the Law, Special Issue: Training and Career Options,* 8(3), 205–216.

Pruett, K. D., & Solnit, A. J. (1998). Psychological and ethical considerations in the preparation of the mental health professional as expert witness. In S. J. Ceci & H. Hembrooke, (Eds.), *Expert witnesses in child abuse case: What can and should be said in court* (pp. 123–136). Washington, DC: American Psychological Association.

WEB RESOURCES

Career Resources in the Forensic Sciences: An Annotated Bibliography
http://www.lib.jjay.cuny.edu/research/foscbib.html

Association of State and Provincial Psychology Boards: Information for Students
http://www.asppb.org/Main/students.asp

Careers in Psychology and Law
http://www.unl.edu/ap-ls/careers.htm

Forensic Psychology Careers and Training
http://psychology.about.com/cs/lawcareer/index.htm

Careers in Forensic Psychology
http://www.wcupa.edu/_ACADEMICS/sch_cas.psy/Career_Paths/Forensic/
Career08.htm

Graduate School Options for Psychology Majors
http://www.psywww.com/careers/options.htm

About Graduate School
http://gradschool.about.com

References

Actkinson, T. R. (2000). Master's and myth: Little-known information about a popular degree. *Eye on Psi Chi, 4*(2), 19–21, 23, 25.

American Association of Political Consultants. (n.d.). *What is the AAPC?* Retrieved on August 15, 2002, at http://www.theaapc.org/what.html

American Board of Forensic Psychology & American Psychology-Law Society (1995). *Petition for the recognition of a specialty in professional psychology.* Retrieved on February 18, 2002, at http://www.unl.edu/ap-ls/petition.PDF

American Psychological Association. (1994). Guidelines for child custody evaluations in divorce proceedings. *American Psychologist, 49,* 677–680.

American Psychological Association (2001). *APA Council of Representative Minutes: August 23 and 26, 2001.* Retrieved on July 29, 2002 at http://members.apa.org/governance/council/01aug_minutes.html

American Psychological Association. (2002). *APA Congressional Fellowship Program.* Retrieved on August 15, 2002 at http://www.apa.org/ppo/funding/congfell.html

American Psychology-Law Society (1998). *Careers and Training in Psychology and Law.* Retrieved on March 15, 2002 at http://www.unl.edu/ap-ls/CAREERS.htm

Anson, R. H., & Bloom, M. E. (1988). Police stress in an occupational context. *Journal of Police Science and Administration, 16,* 229–235.

Appelbaum, P. S., & Grisso, T. (1995). The MacArthur Treatment Competence Study I: Mental illness and competence to consent to treatment. *Law and Human Behavior, 19,* 105–126.

Auguste, R. M., Wicherski, M., & Kohout, J. L. (1999). *1996 master's specialists, and related degrees employment survey.* Retrieved on March 16, 2002, at http://research.apa.org/mes96contents.html

Balser, R. B. (2000). Psychologist-legislator: Reflection on the first year in office. *Professional Psychology: Research & Practice, 31*(5), 473–474.

Bartol, C. R. (1996). Police psychology then, now, and beyond. *Criminal Justice and Behavior, 23,* 70–89.

Bartol, C. R., & Bartol, A. M. (1999). History of forensic psychology. In A. K. Hess & I. B. Weiner (Eds.), *Handbook of forensic psychology* (pp. 3–23). New York: Wiley.

Bergen, G. T., Aceto, R. T., & Chadziewicz, M. M. (1992). Job satisfaction of police psychologists. *Criminal Justice & Behavior Special Issue: Psychology of Policing, 9*(3), 314–329.

Bersoff, D. N., Goodman-Delahunty, J., & Grisso, J. (1997). Training in law and psychology: Models from the Villanova conference. *American Psychologist, 52*(12), 1301–1310.

Blanchard, J. (2002). At home in a strange land! *Professional Psychology: Research & Practice, 33*(3), 285–288.

Boothby, J. L., & Clements, C. B. (2000). A national survey of correctional psychologists. *Criminal Justice & Behavior, 27*(6), 716–732.

Boothby, J. L., & Clements, C. B. (2002). Job satisfaction of correctional psychologists: Implications for recruitment and retention. *Professional Psychology: Research & Practice, 33*(3), 310–315.

Bow, J. N., & Quinnell, F. A. (2001). Psychologists' current practices and procedures in child custody evaluations: Five years after American Psychological Association guidelines. *Professional Psychology: Research & Practice, 32*(3), 261–268.

Brigham, J. C. (1999). What is forensic psychology, anyway? *Law & Human Behavior, 23*(3), 273–298.

Brodsky, C. M. (1982). Work stress in correctional institutions. *Journal of Prison and Jail Health, 2,* 74–102.

Bruck, M. (1998). The trials and tribulations of a novice expert witness. In S. J. Ceci & H. Hembrooke, (Eds.), *Expert witnesses in child abuse cases: What can and should be said in court* (pp. 85–104). Washington, DC: American Psychological Association.

Buffmire, J. A. (1995). Are politics for you? *Professional Psychology: Research & Practice, 26*(5), 453–455.

Bureau of Labor Statistics (2002). *Occupational outlook handbook edition.* Retrieved February 1, 2002, at http://stats.bls.gov/oco/ocoiab.htm

Chappelle, W., & Rosengren, K. (2001). Maintaining composure and credibility as an expert witness during cross-examination. *Journal of Forensic Psychology Practice, 1*(3), 51–67.

Chronicle of Higher Education (2001). *Average salaries for full-time faculty members, 2000–2001.* Retrieved on March 15, 2002, at http://chronicle.com/weekly/v47/i32/32a01901.htm

Cooper, A. (2002). Harris called "Mediation King". *Richmond Times Dispatch.* Retrieved on August 1, 2002, at http://216.239.51.100/search?q=cache:Zw6YIKa3qxkC:www.timesdispatch.com/business/more/MGBDKF31S2D.html

DeAngelis, T. (2001). A different kind of practice. *Monitor on Psychology, 32*(2). Retrieved on August, 15, 2002, at http://www.apa.org/monitor/feb01/careerpath2.html

Delprino, R. P., & Bahn C. (1988). National survey of the extent and nature of psychological services in police departments. *Professional Psychology: Research & Practice, 19*(4), 421–425.

DiVasto, P.V. (1985). Measuring the aftermath of rape. *Journal of Psychosocial Nursing and Mental Health Services, 23,* 33–35.

Ferrell, S. W., Morgan, R. D., & Winterowd, C. L. (2000). Job satisfaction of mental health professionals providing group psychotherapy in state correctional facilities. *International Journal of Offender Therapy and Comparative Criminology, 44,* 232–241.

Fowler, R. D. (1996). Psychology, public policy, and the Congressional Fellowship program. In R. P. Lorion, I. Iscoe, P.H. Deleon, & G. R. VandenBos (Eds.), *Psychology and public policy: Balancing public service and professional need* (pp. ix–xiv). Washington, DC: American Psychological Association.

Glassman, J. B. (1998). Preventing and managing board complaints: The downside risk of custody evaluation. *Professional Psychology: Research & Practice, 29*(2), 121–124.

Hafemeister, T. L., Ogloff, J. R., & Small, M. A. (1990). Training and careers in law and psychology: The perspective of students and graduates of dual degree programs. *Behavioral Sciences & the Law, Special Issue: Training and Career Options, 8*(3), 263–283.

Harris, G. T., Rice, M. E., & Quinsey, V. L. (1993). Violent recidivism of mental disordered offenders: The development of a statistical prediction instrument. *Criminal Justice and Behavior, 20,* 315–335.

Hawk, K. M. (1997). Personal reflections on a career in correctional psychology. *Professional Psychology: Research and Practice, 28*(4), 335–337.

Hays-Thomas, R. L. (2000). The silent conversation: Talking about the master's degree. *Professional Psychology: Research and Practice, 31,* 339–345.

Heilbrun, A. B. (1999). Recommending probation and parole. In A. K. Hess & I. B. Weiner (Eds.), *The handbook of forensic psychology* (pp. 303–349). New York: Wiley.

Hess, A. K. (1998). Accepting forensic case referrals: Ethical and professional considerations. *Professional Psychology: Research & Practice, 29*(2), 109–114.

Hess, A. K. (1999). Defining forensic psychology. In A. K. Hess & I. B. Weiner (Eds.), *The handbook of forensic psychology* (pp. 24–47). New York: Wiley.

Hoge, D., Poythress, N., Bonnie, R., Monahamn, J., Eisenberg, M., & Feucht-Haviar, T. (1997). The MacArthur Adjudication Competence Study: Diagnosis, psychopathology, and adjudicative competence-related abilities. *Behavioral Sciences and the Law, 15,* 329–345.

Huss, M. T. (2001). What is forensic psychology? It's not *Silence of the Lambs! Eye on Psi Chi, 5*(3), 25–27.

Kassin, S. M., & Wrightsman, L. S. (1983). The construction and validation of a Juror Bias Scale. *Journal of Research in Personality, 17,* 423–442.

Kennemer, W. N. (1995). Psychology and the political process. *Professional Psychology: Research & Practice, 26*(5), 456–458.

Kirkland, K., & Kirkland, K. L. (2001). Frequency of child custody evaluation complaints and related disciplinary action: A survey of the Association of State and Provincial Psychology Boards. *Professional Psychology: Research & Practice, 32*(2), 171–174.

Kravitz, D. A., Cutler, B. L., & Brock, P. (1993). Reliability and validity of the original and revised Legal Attitudes Questionnaire. *Law and Human Behavior, 17,* 661–677.

Kuther, T. L. (1999). Competency to provide informed consent in older adulthood. *Gerontology and Geriatrics Education, 20*(1), 15–30.

Kuther, T. L. (2003). *The psychology major's handbook.* Pacific Grove, CA: Wadsworth

Kuther, T. L., & Morgan, R. (2004). *Extending the boundaries of psychology: Career opportunities in a changing world.* Pacific Grove, CA: Wadsworth.

Laboratory for Community Psychiatry. (1974). *Competency to stand trial and mental illness.* Northvale, NJ: Jason Aronson.

Levant, R. F., Moldawsky, S., & Stigall, T. T. (2000). The evolving profession of psychology: Comment on Hays-Thomas' (2000) "The silent conversation." *Professional Psychology Research and Practice, 31,* 346–348.

Levant, R. F., Reed, G. M., Ragusea, S. A., DiCowden, M., Murphy, M. J., Sullivan, F., Craig, P. L., & Stout, C. E. (2001). Envisioning and accessing new roles for professional psychology. *Professional Psychology: Research & Practice, 32*(1) 79–87

Lipsitt, P. D., Lelos, D., & McGarry. A. I. (1971). Competency for trial: A screening instrument. *American Journal of Psychiatry, 128,* 105–109.

Lloyd, M. A. (1997). *Graduate school options for psychology majors.* Retrieved on August 21, 2002, at http://www.psywww.com/careers/options.htm

Lloyd-Bostock, S. (1988). The benefits of legal psychology: Possibilities, practice and dilemmas. *British Journal of Psychology, 79,* 417–440.

Marxsen, D., Yuille, J. C., & Nisbet, M. (1995). The complexities of eliciting and assessing children's statements. *Psychology, Public Policy, and Law, 1,* 450–460.

Max, D. T. (2000, December). The cop and the therapist. *The New York Times Magazine,* p. 94.

Milan, M. A., Chin, C. E., & Nguyen, Z. X. (1999). Practicing psychology in correctional settings: Assessment, treatment, and substance abuse programs. In A. K. Hess & I. B. Weiner (Eds.), *The handbook of forensic psychology* (pp. 580–602). New York: Wiley.

Mobley, M. J. (1999). Psychotherapy with criminal offenders. In A. K. Hess & I. B. Weiner (Eds.), *The handbook of forensic psychology* (pp. 603–639). New York: Wiley.

Morgan, R. D., Winterowd, C. L., & Ferrell, S. W. (1999). A national survey of group psychotherapy services in correctional facilities. *Professional Psychology: Research and Practice, 30,* 600–606.

Murray, B. (1998, January). Ph.D.s apply talents to emerging careers. *Monitor on Psychology.* Retrieved on July 31, 2002, at http://www.apa.org/monitor/jan98/phd.html

Myers, B., & Arena, M. P. (2001). Trial consultation: A new direction in applied psychology. *Professional Psychology: Research and Practice, 32,* 386–391.

Nietzel, M. T., & Dillehay, R. C. (1986). *Psychological consultation in the courtroom.* New York: Pergamon.

O'Connor, M., Sales, B. D., & Shulman, D. (1996). Mental health professional expertise in the courtroom. In B. D. Sales & D. W. Shulma (Eds.), *Law, mental health, and mental disorder* (pp. 40–60). Pacific Grove, CA: Brooks/Cole.

Ogloff, J. R. P. (1999). Law and human behavior: Reflecting back and looking forward. *Law and Human Behavior, 23*(1), 1–7.

Ogloff, J. R. P. (2000). Two steps forward and one step backward: The law and psychology movement(s) in the 20th century. *Law & Human Behavior, 24*(4).

Ogloff, J. R. P., Beavers, D. J., & DeLeon, P. H. (1999). Psychology and the law: A shared vision for the 21st century. *Professional Psychology: Research and Practice, 30,* 331–332.

Ogloff, J. R. P., & Cronshaw, S. F. (2001). Expert psychological testimony: Assisting or misleading the trier of fact? *Canadian Psychology, 42,* 87–91.

Ogloff, J. R. P., Roberts, C. F., & Roesch, R. (1993). The insanity defense: Legal standards and clinical assessment. *Applied and Preventative Psychology, 2,* 163–178.

Ogloff, J. R. P., Tomkins, A. J., & Bersoff, D. N. (1996). Education and training in psychology and law/criminal justice: Historical foundations, present structures, and future developments. *Criminal Justice & Behavior, 23*(1), 200–235.

Otto, R. K., & Heilbrun, K. (2002). The practice of forensic psychology: A look toward the future in light of the past. *American Psychologist, 57,* 5–18.

Otto, R. K., Heilbrun, K. G., & Thomas (1990). Training and credentialing in forensic psychology. *Behavioral Sciences & the Law, Special Issue: Training and career options,* 8(3), 217–231.

Pamintuan, T. (2000). Spin doctor. *1099: The Magazine for Independent Professionals.* Retrieved on August 15, 2002, at http://www.1099.com/c/ar/di/SpinDoctor_d035.html

Reid, W. H. (1999). The top 19 things to remember when working with lawyers and courts. *Journal of Practical Psychology and Behavioral Health.* Retrieved on August 15, 2002, at http://www.reidpsychiatry.com/columns/Reid07-99.pdf

Roediger, H. (1997). Teaching, research, and more: Psychologists in an academic career. In R. J. Sternberg (Ed.), *Career paths in psychology: Where your degree can take you* (pp. 7–30). Washington, DC: American Psychological Association.

Rogers, R. (1984). *Rogers Criminal Responsibility Assessment Scales (R-CRAS) and test manual.* Odess, FL: Psychological Assessment Resources.

Rotgers, F., & Barrett, D. (1996). *Daubert v. Merrell Dow* and expert testimony by clinical psychologists: Implications and recommendations for practice. *Professional Psychology: Research and Practice, 27,* 467–474.

Ruch, L. O., Gartrell. J. W. M., Amedeo, S. R., & Coyne, B. J. (1991). The Sexual Assault Symptoms Scale: Measuring self-reported sexual assault trauma in the emergency room. *Psychological Assessment, 3,* 3–8.

Ruch, L. O., Gartrell, J.W., Ramelli, A., & Coyne, B. (1991). The Clinical Trauma Assessment: Evaluating sexual assault victims in the emergency room. *Psychological Assessment, 3,* 405–411.

Salzinger, K. (1995). The academic life. *Psychological Science Agenda.* Retrieved on August 7, 2002, at http://www.apa.org/psa/janfeb95/acad.html

Scrivner, E. M., & Kurke, M. I. (1995). Police psychology at the dawn of the 21st century. In M. I. Kurke & E. M. Scrivner (Eds.), *Police psychology into the 21st century,* (pp. 3–30). Hillsdale, NJ: Erlbaum.

Selkin, J. (1994). Psychological autopsy: Scientific psychohistory or clinical intuition? *American Psychologist, 49,* 74–75.

Shneidman, E. S. (1994). The psychological autopsy. *American Psychologist, 49,* 75–76.

Sorensen, J. L., Masson, C. L., Clark, W. W., & Morin, S. F. (1998). Providing public testimony: A guide for psychologists. *Professional Psychology: Research & Practice, 29*(6), 588–593.

Stapp, J. (1996). An interesting career in psychology: Trial consultant. *Psychological Science Agenda.* Retrieved on August 15, 2002, at http://www.apa.org/science/ic-stapp.html

Streier, F. (1999). Whither trial consulting? Issues and projections. *Law and Human Behavior, 23*, 93–115.

Strickland, T. (1996). Moving psychology toward (self) recognition as a public resource: The views of a congressman psychologist. In R. P. Lorion, I. Iscoe, P.H. Deleon, & G. R. VandenBos (Eds.), *Psychology and public policy: Balancing public service and professional need* (pp. 369–389). Washington, DC: American Psychological Association.

Studebaker, C. A., & Penrod, S. D. (1997). Pretrial publicity: The media, the law, and common sense. *Psychology, Public Policy, and Law, 3*, 93–115.

Sullivan, M. J. (2001). Psychologists as legislators: Results of the 2000 elections. *Professional Psychology: Research and Practice, 32*, 40–43.

Super, J. T. (1999). Forensic psychology and law enforcement. In A. K. Hess & I. B. Weiner (Eds.), *The handbook of forensic psychology* (pp. 409–439). New York: Wiley.

Tremper, C. R. (1987). Organized psychology's efforts to influence judicial policy-making. *American Psychologist, 42*(5), 496–501.

Trull, T. J., & Phares, E. J. (2001). *Clinical psychology.* Pacific Grove, CA: Wadsworth.

Vesilind, P. A. (2000). *So you want to be a professor? A handbook for graduate students.* Thousand Oaks, CA: Sage.

Vincent, T. A. (1990). A view from the Hill: The human element in policy making on Capitol Hill. *American Psychologist, 45*(1), 61–64.

Walker, L. E. (1990). Psychological assessment of sexually abused children for legal evaluation and expert witness testimony. *Professional Psychology: Research & Practice, 21*(5), 344–353.

Webster, C. D., Harris, G. T., Rice, M. E., Cormier, C., & Quinsey, V. L. (1994). *The violence prediction scheme: Assessing dangerousness in high risk men.* Toronto: University of Toronto, Centre of Criminology.

Williams, S., Wicherski, M., & Kohout, J. L. (2000). *Salaries in psychology 1999: Report of the 1999 APA salary survey.* Washington, D.C.: American Psychological Association

Wrightsman, L. S. (2001). *Forensic psychology.* Belmont, CA: Wadsworth.

Wrightsman, L. S., Greene, E., Neitzel, M. T., & Fortune, W. H. (2002). *Psychology and the Legal System.* Belmont, CA: Wadsworth.

Index

Academic careers. See College and University Professors. See Research Careers.
Aceto, R. T., 4, 33, 76
Ackerman, M. J., 22
Actkinson, T. R., 64, 75
Advice for students
    And correctional psychology, 32
    And expert witness, 46
    And forensic psychology, 14, 21-22, 24, 50, 70-71
    And police psychology, 34
    And policy, 61, 54-55
Advocacy. See Policy.
Amedeo, S. R., 18, 79
American Academy of Forensic Psychology, 5
American Association for Correctional Psychology, 35
American Association of Correctional Psychologists, 5
American Association of Political Consultants, 56, 75
American Board of Forensic Psychology, 6, 22, 75
American College of Forensic Psychology, 5
American Psychological Association (APA), 5, 6, 10, 11, 18, 21, 36, 48, 52, 54, 58, 75
American Psychological Association Congressional Fellow, 54-55
American Psychology-Law Society, 5, 6, 9, 75
American Society of Trial Consultants, 48
amicus curiae, 52
Anson, R. H., 33, 75
Appelbaum, P. S., 19, 75
Appelgate, D., 56
Arena, M. P., 42, 43, 44, 48, 78
Arrigo, B. A., 9
Assessment
adjudicative competence, 13, 16, 17, 25-26, 49

child abuse, 16, 18, 21
child custody, 3, 18-19,
competence, 2, 16, 19
criminal responsibility, 13, 16-17, 25-26
    fitness for duty, 4, 33
    forensic. See Forensic Evaluation
    in correctional settings, 30
    neuropsychological, 3, 16
    personal and emotional injury, 3, 19
    psychological autopsy, 20
    risk for violence, 2, 3, 13, 19, 20, 23, 30, 50
    selection of CIA agents, 37
    selection of police officers, 4, 32-33
    victim trauma and injury, 3, 16, 18, 19-20
Attorney
    And forensic evaluation, 16, 17, 23, 24, 27, 49
    And expert witness, 45
    And trial consultants, 4, 42-44
    Challenges of working with, 24, 27, 46-47
    Statistics on, 44
Auguste, R. M., 32, 75

Bachelor's level careers, 71-72
Bahn, C., 32, 76
Balser, R. B., 75
Barrett, D., 46, 79
Bartol, A. M., 5, 75
Bartol, C. R., 4, 5, 32, 33, 34, 35, 75,
Beavers, D. J., 3, 78
Bennett, C. E., 48
Bergen, G. T., 4, 33, 76
Bersoff, D. N., 67, 76, 79
Blanchard, J., 76
Blau, T. H., 35
Bloom, M. E., 33, 75
Bonnie, R., 77
Boothby, J. L., 4, 30, 31, 32, 35, 76
Bow, J. N., 19, 76
Brigham, J. C., 5, 6, 76

Nietzel, M. T., 17, 42, 43, 44, 46, 47, 48, 78, 80
Nisbet, M., 18, 78
Nordal, K., 57

O'Connor, M., 16, 78
Ogloff, J. R., 3, 16, 17, 67, 68, 69, 70, 72, 77, 78, 79
Otto, R. K., 5, 68, 69

Pamintuan, T., 56, 79
Penrod, S. D., 42, 80
Petrila, J., 22
Ph.D. (doctor of philosophy), 66. Also see Doctoral Degrees.
Phares, E. J., 10, 80
Plaintiff, 19
Police officers
   and fitness for duty evaluations, 4, 33
   and operational support, 33
   counseling of, 4, 33
   organizational development, 33
   selection and training of, 4, 32-33
Police psychologists
   advantages and disadvantages of, 33-34, 39-40
   job market for, 34
   job satisfaction and, 34
   roles and responsibilities of, 4, 32-33, 36-37
   salaries and income of, 34
   training tips, 34
Police psychology. Also see Police Psychologists.
   definition 32-33
   web resources, 35
Policy career
   advantages and disadvantages of, 53-54, 55, 60-61
   roles and responsibilities, 5, 52-54, 58-60
   salaries and income, 54
   training tips, 61
Policy
   definition, 52
   fellowship, 5, 58-60
   organizations and think tanks 53-54
   psychology and 52
   research, 5, 52-54, 58, 60
   web resources 57
Political consultant, 5, 56

Political psychology, 57
Politics, 5, 54, 56, 58
Poynter, D., 48
Poythress, N. G., 22, 77
Practice
   and licensure, 21-22
   and mediation, 45
   clinical practice (see clinical practice)
   private practice, 20, 23, 25, 26,36, 39, 48, 49
   professional practice, 6, 21, 23, 32
   research and, 3
Prison. See Correctional Ssettings.
Probation, 31, 35
Program development and evaluation, 2, 4, 30, 54, 57
Pruett, K. D., 72
Psy.D. (doctor of psychology), 66. See also Doctoral Degrees.
Psychological autopsy, 20
Psychologists. See Graduate-level Careers, Psychology.
Psychology
   and APA specialty status, 11
   clinical psychology, 6, 12, 23, 24, 25, 32, 34, 36
   counseling psychology, 5, 21, 32, 34
   definition, 2
   developmental psychology, 58, 60, 65, 70
   experimental psychology, 44, 65, 70
   forensic psychology. See Forensic Psychology.
   legal psychology. See Legal Psychology, Psychology and Law.
   role in the legal system 2-3
   social psychology, 10, 44, 65, 68, 69, 70
Psychology and law
   current issues, 5-6, 11
   definition, 2, 5-6
   interface, 2-3, 47
   web resources, 9-10
Psychology career. See Bachelor's level Careers, Graduate-level Careers.
Psychotherapy. See Treatment.
Public attitudes, 5, 42, 44, 56
Public policy. See Policy.

Quinnell, F. A., 19, 76
Quinsey, V. L., 19, 77, 80